Midwest Canoe Trails

John W. Malo

Produced by Greatlakes Living Press
of Waukegan, Illinois,
for Contemporary Books, Inc.

 Contemporary Books, Inc.
Chicago

Library of Congress Cataloging in Publication Data

Malo, John W
   Midwest canoe trails.

   Includes index.
   1. Canoes and canoeing—Middle West—Guide-books.
   2. Canoes and canoeing—Ontario—Guide-books.
   3. Middle West—Description and travel—Guide-books.
   4. Ontario—Description and travel—Guide-books.
   I. Title.
   GV776.M53M34 1978   917.7   77-91182
   ISBN 0-8092-7680-1
   ISBN 0-8092-7679-8 pbk.

Published by Contemporary Books, Inc.
180 North Michigan Avenue, Chicago, Illinois 60601
Manufactured in the United States of America
Library of Congress Catalog Card Number: 77-91182
International Standard Book Number: 0-8092-7680-1 (cloth)
                                    0-8092-7679-8 (paper)

Published simultaneously in Canada by
Beaverbooks
953 Dillingham Road
Pickering, Ontario L1W 1Z7
Canada

To the many experienced canoeists who promote the sport in multitudinous ways and who could have written this book had they the time to travel the miles to far-flung waters, engage in the necessary correspondence, and conduct dialogues with state and local officials—to them this book is affectionately dedicated.

Also by John W. Malo

Canoeing (for children)

Malo's Complete Guide to Canoeing & Canoe-Camping
(Also in paperback)

Wilderness Canoeing

All-Terrain Adventure Vehicles

Houseboating Guide

Motor-Camping Around Europe

Tranquil Trails (a nature diary)

Contents

1

Prelude to Paddling Midwestern Waters

In all probability there is no region in the world that offers so much canoeable water over such an extensive area and so readily available to millions of people as does the upper Midwest of the United States and the contiguous province of Ontario, Canada.

The Midwest offers enormous variety to the canoeist. As well as varied courses of moving water, there are chains of connected lakes, bordered by natural banks that range from flatland cornfields to bracken fern lying under northern conifers.

This treasureland of canoe trails is rich in history, inviting the canoeist who explores its waters to contemplate the days when the land belonged to the American Indian. The spirit of these peoples beckons us to enjoy the waters, experience the joy of their light birchbark designs and ride the currents under our own power. The Midwest's legendary waters knew, in sequence, the paddle of the American

Indian, the voyageur, the fur trader, the missionary, and the pioneer. And up to this space-age day some midwestern water trails retain traces of their primitive mystique for us to experience, enjoy, and, many times, challenge.

The 1870s era of the fur trade, here depicted in "Shooting a Rapid," from an engraving by Frances Ann Hopkins. (Minnesota Historical Society)

For the water adventurer there is not a more efficient craft than the canoe: pointed at both ends, it is easily propelled as it parts the water at the bow and allows it to return at the stern without wake or disturbance. The canoe requires but several inches of water depth for flotation, making it possible to explore water trails where no other watercraft dare venture. In it you can ride out the heavy seas of open water, and you can also explore feeder streams and creeks, the backoffs and bayous of rivers, and the rock-strewn coves and bays of lakes—places seldom seen by the average outdoor enthusiast.

In a canoe you will capture an intimacy with the silence and isolation of nature and become attuned to age-old rhythms. You will know the contemplative moment, be able to strip life of nonessentials, and experience the satisfaction of moving from one place to another by your own muscle. Once at your destination, you will savor the joy of accomplishment, of finding a haven from the pressures you had left—way back there.

In planning a paddling itinerary in the Midwest, canoeists are limited in scope only by their ability, time, and imagination. From brief interludes—one-day excursions and overnight adventures—to lengthy vacation cruises and far-flung wilderness trips, midwestern waters present a variety of water experiences that assures a continuing challenge.

In selecting the rivers for inclusion in this book, several general guidelines were followed. Rivers not included were those with capricious water levels, especially those that are low during the summer canoeing season; rivers with lazy, low-quality water where only carp and suckers thrive; those with large expanses of lowland with dense water plant growth and brushy banks; and those that do not offer the contrasts of nature that canoeists relish. And because the participants uppermost in mind were the wide range of canoeists below the expert class—beginners, youngsters, oldsters— the competitive level whitewater rivers were not included.

In addition, many rivers that certainly meet the above considerations had to be omitted because of lack of space. As veteran canoeists know, there is enough material for an entire book in almost any river. If your favorite river is missing, please accept our apology.

Your canoe trips will go more smoothly if you get into the habit of seeking out enthusiastic resource persons. These can be local associates, canoe club members, or livery personnel; in remote canoe country, they can be outfitters, guides, game wardens, forest rangers or Canadian Mounties. These on-the-spot individuals will clue you in to water conditions, campsites, the local insect situation and effective repellents, and other information that will assure a successful outing. Advance knowledge is essential. Take fences, for example. When canoeing in the Midwest, one must expect to come upon fences strung across streams. It therefore becomes necessary to develop the ability to avoid being swept broadside into a fence on a strong current before a proper passing strategy can be determined. This can be accomplished by keeping a sharp lookout ahead and, when a fence is spotted, heading shoreward where the current is more moderate. Then, keeping the craft parallel to the shore, the bowman lifts the fence and ducks under, followed by the sternman as the canoe is pulled through. If it is impossible to raise the fence, the canoe must be portaged.

If you choose to join one of the many groups that sponsor organized canoe trips, the group will usually assume responsibility for arranging a shuttle system. If you canoe on your own, however, whether in one or two canoes, the following method works quite well. After the trip is over, have one member hike back to the car. A hiker with a canoe paddle in hand is a familiar sight in canoe country and can easily get a ride with local residents or tourists. The rest of the party can wait it out at a store, gas station, or farmhouse. There is also the possibility of approaching a motorist and offering to pay for the service of having your party and equipment transported. Rural teenagers are especially amenable to this type of offer. There is the added benefit that in the process of getting back to your car you often meet interesting people, and interacting with them can add another dimension to a canoeing adventure.

For most rivers covered in this text, bridges that span your canoe route are indicated. The reasons are valid. Should something adverse occur, such as bad weather or a broken paddle, or if the party wishes to shorten the planned trip, one or more members of the party can make their way to the nearest bridge to flag down a motorist for help. Again, one should always carry the identifying paddle.

When planning to paddle a river below a power dam, ascertain the hours of water release. At those times the water level rises perceptibly and this could adversely affect both the paddling schedule and a low-lying campsite, such as those situated on islands or low banks.

When waters are running high and fast and you wish to stop on a rise to rest, eat lunch, or camp, be extremely cautious. Snakes and other animals also seek out high ground when their domains are threatened by rising waters.

When river cruising, portages must be spotted early enough for an efficient and safe takeout. Even when on a strange river you can spot a portage in many ways: a break in the tree line or shoreline groundcover; a well-trod, smooth path leading to the water's edge; and many times a tall sapling or post marker is visible. Once ashore, stay with the portage path, no matter how circuitous it seems. Most modern portages originated with the Indians, and they, as we, did not wish to take unnecessary steps.

As you use this guide, keep in mind that there are many variables involved; moving watercourses are constantly fluctuating, and conditions can change from year to year, month to month, and even day to day. Observations gained today may not be valid tomorrow. To insure the success of a canoe trip, consider such factors as length of the proposed trip in relation to the experience of trippers, adequate food and water supply, and protection from the elements and insects. Practically all of the canoe trails discussed here will provide a safe and satisfying trip for the beginner when in the company of an experienced canoeist.

Unpleasant canoeing experiences, most of which are preventable, come about in many ways. These include factors such as improper canoe balance, inadequate freeboard, personal fatigue, haste, overestimating one's ability, and underestimating the power of the wind and moving water. These natural and personal factors can spoil an outing. Neither the author nor the publisher is liable for accidents that may occur due to errors or omissions in this book. Each canoeist must be responsible for thoroughly checking each trail before embarking. It is also incumbent upon each canoeist to have all the necessary safety equipment and to use common sense while on the water.

A canoe trail guide with voluminous wordage about accesses, boulders in the water, mileage, takeouts, and so on, could be quite dry and boring. So in the belief that modern canoeists are the elite of the watercraft world, broad in interests, this book will include the interweaving of history, geology, biology, natural history, and local color. After all, there is much more to the enjoyment of canoeing than paddling, looking straight ahead, and thinking about the next meal, portage, or takeout point.

Most modern canoeists are nature lovers and conservationists, sensitive to the ecology of this interesting world of ours. They do not leave their mark on riverbeds or shores by adding to the approximately 65 billion nonreturnable bottles and cans of litter. A marsh marigold in bloom is not enhanced by a rosary of pull-tab can openers encircling it. As beneficiaries of a great midwestern canoeing heritage, we must be dedicated to the obligation to safeguard and cherish the watercourses and shorelines for future generations that they too, as we, will know the joy of skimming over and identifying with the eternal waters.

Explanatory Notes

In discussing canoe trail access, all roads will be indicated by the title "Route" followed by a number. By referring to a state highway map, the reader can learn whether the route number refers to a local road, a state or U.S. highway, or an interstate highway.

Due to the fluctuations in the economy, no prices are quoted in the book. It is suggested that you query the various sources for publications and guides and for rental, camping, and launching fees.

Place no significance on the order in which the rivers of various states are discussed, as no priority is intended.

2

Adventure Trails of Illinois

The comparatively level plain of Illinois, innervated by many waterways, served well the Indian tribes of Illini, Iroquois, Potawatomi, and others with adequate water, fertile soil, and a temperate climate. The land supported abundant crops of maize, pumpkin, squash, berries, nuts, and fruit. The waters offered migratory ducks and geese, fish, turtles, frogs, crayfish, mussels, and so on when the need arose to augment the Indians' food needs.

There was a harmonious relationship between the numerous water trails and the Indian bark canoe, which offered great mobility throughout the area. The Indian tribes moved with ease, as did the European explorers when they came upon the scene. As early as 1673 Father Pere Marquette, S.J., and Louis Jolliet entered Illinois country with birchbark canoes and Indian guides. On the 300th anniversary of their trip, in 1973, it was reenacted by seven expert canoeists in a prodigious 2,900-mile, four-month celebration. The reenactment was made in two twenty-foot Algonquin style birchbarks. The crew members were garbed in the clothing of the 1670s, assuming the roles of Louis Jolliet, Father Marquette, and five other explorers. Their route followed the original course: from St. Ignace on the north shore of Lake Michigan to Green Bay, Wisconsin; down the Fox, Wisconsin, and Mississippi rivers to the site of the Akamsea Indian village in Arkansas. The return trip was via the Mississippi, Illinois, and Des Plaines rivers and the Chicago portage to Lake Michigan and Green Bay.

On April 14, 1968, canoeists recreated the 1675 journey of Father Jacques Marquette, arriving in Ottawa, Illinois, after paddling down the Illinois River from Marseilles. Father Marquette celebrated the first Christian service to the Indians at the site of the present-day Starved Rock Park. These canoes, simulated birchbark replicas of the original, are popular in many contemporary celebrations of historical events.
(*Chicago Tribune* photo)

In 1675 Father Marquette founded a mission at the Indian village of Kaskaskia, near the present site of Utica, Illinois. In 1680 LaSalle, in the company of three Recollect Fathers, established Fort Creve Coeur, near present-day Lake Peoria. Other explorers, missionaries and settlers established missions and settlements at Fort Chartres in 1720 and at Prairie du Rocher in 1722.

These bits of history indicate a few of the permanent

footholds established by explorers—all made possible by the canoe.

Illinois Canoe Trails

The water cycle being indestructible, today you can paddle the same Illinois water as did the early voyagers long before the Declaration of Independence was ratified. Several years after Father Marquette and Louis Jolliet visited Illinois in 1673, Henri de Tonti, a member of Robert Cavelier de LaSalle's expedition, described Illinois as ". . . the most beautiful country in the world, abounding in fruits, berries, animals and birds. . . . " Present-day canoeists are denied the sight of wild turkey and buffalo, but they can enjoy the shorelines while being borne on placid waters and experiencing some of the tracings of history. Illinois canoe trails offer a wide variety of trips on rivers that have their own individual character and heritage of song and story.

Fox River

From time immemorial the Fox River Valley has been rich in natural resources. It was ardently embraced by the native Indians, serving well the Miami and Fox tribes and, at various other times, the Algonquins, Iroquois, and other tribes, too. Today the valley serves modern men and women with a dependable water resource, and is the scene of farming, mining, parks, vacation homes, fishing, and boating.

The Fox flows from Wisconsin through the "Chain-of-Lakes" region and ninety-five miles later joins the Illinois River. Its entire length is good canoeing water. The stream has a slow current and a fairly uniform depth averaging about two to four feet, with a maximum depth of ten feet in certain stretches.

Except for Chain-of-Lakes State Park, there are no facilities for overnight camping on the upper Fox. However, motels and hotels abound in the towns and marinas along

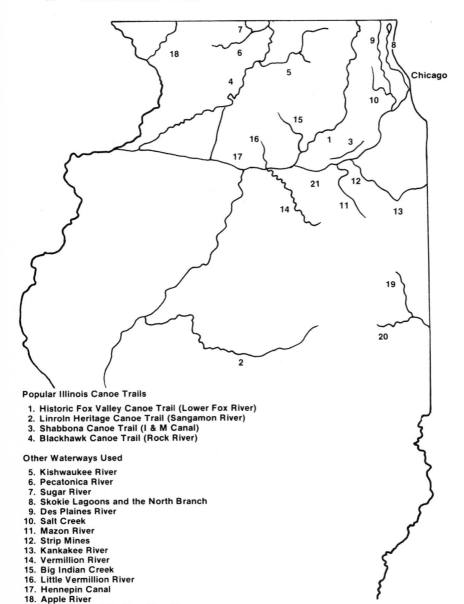

Popular Illinois Canoe Trails

1. Historic Fox Valley Canoe Trail (Lower Fox River)
2. Linroln Heritage Canoe Trail (Sangamon River)
3. Shabbona Canoe Trail (I & M Canal)
4. Blackhawk Canoe Trail (Rock River)

Other Waterways Used

5. Kishwaukee River
6. Pecatonica River
7. Sugar River
8. Skokie Lagoons and the North Branch
9. Des Plaines River
10. Salt Creek
11. Mazon River
12. Strip Mines
13. Kankakee River
14. Vermillion River
15. Big Indian Creek
16. Little Vermillion River
17. Hennepin Canal
18. Apple River
19. Middle Fork of the Vermillion River
20. Salt Fork of the Vermillion River
21. Illinois River

the river. Food supplies or restaurant meals can be obtained at any of the towns and at some of the taverns along the river.

Should you opt for a Chain-of-Lakes trip, you can put in at Oak Point State Park, on Route 173 a bit west of Antioch. A short paddle southward is Chain-of-Lakes State Park, where another public ramp is available. Beyond these free public access points, Fox and Pistakee lakes have many private launching areas, and the owners charge a fee. Obviously, the bulk of their patronage is from speedboaters.

Fishing the Fox was a rewarding experience in an earlier day; game fish abounded in such lakes as Grass, Fox, Marie, and Pistakee. The river proper also offered stretches of well-stocked water, such as Burton's Bridge, the brush piles and backoffs below Cary, and the deep holes near Plano. Today fishers concentrate their efforts below the dams, and all along the river, bank lines are used, mostly for catfish and carp. The canoeist who wishes to combine paddling and fishing should fish the Fox River before Memorial Day and after Labor Day because between those dates other water recreation, especially speedboating and waterskiing, is very heavy.

Continuing downstream in the river proper past Johnsburg and a short distance below the Route 120 bridge is the McHenry Dam State Park, where canoes may be put in or taken out. The bridge on Route 14 between Cary and Fox River Grove is a good access point with limited parking space for cars on the south side.

The next free access point is at the city park at Algonquin. Launch or take out here on the west bank, north of the bridge. *Do not* attempt to run the Algonquin dam; it has been fatal to several canoeists in the past. At East Dundee there is an access point on the east bank, north of the bridge. There is also a public access point at the Fabian Forest Preserve in Batavia, a few miles downstream. It is an easy day's trip from Elgin to Batavia.

For canoeists interested in geology and the flora of the Fox River Valley, the city park at Batavia presents an interesting outcrop of rock—an upper bed of earthy dolomite, weathered to a buff color, and lower beds of gray dolomite containing a considerable amount of chert. In the southwest part of the park the angular unconformity between the upper and lower beds can be seen. The Batavia Bog is located in an old channel of the Fox River that was formed when the Minooka Glacier blocked the river north of St. Charles. The peat, composed mostly of reed types of vegetation, has a maximum thickness of ten to twelve inches and is relatively coarse and used as a soil conditioner. It is underlain by a deep layer of marl.

After approximately four hours of paddling from Batavia to the launching ramp at the Yorkville dam, canoeists arrive at the most inspiring section of the Fox River. Between Yorkville and Wedron, less than a two-hour drive from the Chicago metropolitan area, is this enchanting example of Illinois heritage, a concentrated mosaic of water, topography, and history. Rarely does one find in a river such a variety of impressive features. Included are the varied color and texture values of field and forest, high bluffs, feeder streams that lead to caves and waterfalls, the Indian battlefield of Maramech Hill, the first known Norwegian settlement, the remnants of an old stone mill, a former sulfur spring spa, five species of evergreen, and many varieties of ferns, mosses, liverworts, and wild flowers. In this seemingly imperishable stretch of the Fox there are no dams, the shoreline retains its integrity, and, with the exception of Wedron, no towns are visible to the paddler. History, nature, nostalgia—all unfold at each stroke of the paddle.

But as you approach Wedron, all is not Camelot in this revered sweep of the Fox River. A 1,000-year-old cedar, claimed to be the oldest living thing in Illinois, was cut down several years ago, supposedly by vandals, and the hills of silica tailings along with the outflow pipe from the

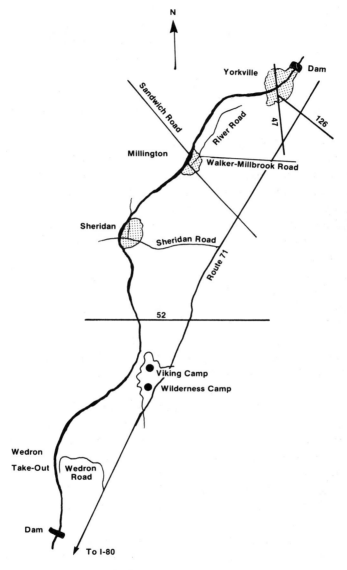

Fox River's most scenic stretch.

quarry of the Wedron Silica Company on the north bank bring the canoeist abruptly back to our age of technology.

Efforts are being made to preserve the beauty of the area, however. Litter is constantly monitored and removed. The Illinois Paddling Council sponsors an annual clean-up trip on this stretch of the river. Supplied with plastic and burlap bags, canoeists are assigned to portions of the river. They collect the refuse, garbage, and litter en route and deposit it in waiting trucks. This ongoing program illustrates that canoeists are actively concerned about the preservation and maintenance of our many waterways. Groups and individuals who cooperate in the effort to maintain quality water for all to use and enjoy include the Izaak Walton League, scout groups, American Youth Hostel, the Sierra Club, the Prairie Club, outdoor clubs, and students.

Takeout is at an old abandoned bridge that has had its floor planking removed. The takeout on the left is private, but Mrs. Stangeland, the owner, lives across the road and readily gives permission when notified and asked.

What better way than the Yorkville-Wedron cruise to introduce canoeing to youth? It served this purpose beautifully for urban young men from the Izaak Walton Outdoor Club of Foreman High School in Chicago. The physical exercise of paddling, first-time observation from a river, and the soft beauty completely enchanted the students, and a tradition was born. Each succeeding year, participation in the October cruise has increased.

Completing the Fox River run to where it empties into the Illinois River requires a portage route. About 150 feet upstream of a weir is the landing and road. Take out the canoe and follow the road across the weir to the levee that separates the river from the sluiceway. Crossing the weir may seem a bit precarious, but the footing is good. The path descends to the levee and back to the foot of the dam. After the put-in you can run the turbulent water below the dam or line the canoes down to more acceptable water.

Vermillion River

There are two Vermillion rivers in Illinois, flowing in opposite directions. The Vermillion to the northwest runs through Livingston and LaSalle counties; the South Vermillion, also noted on some maps as the "Middle Fork," flows southeast through Ford, Champaign, and Vermillion counties. Both rivers are designated on the official highway map of Illinois for easy reference. If you are planning a group canoe trip on one of these rivers, be sure everyone in the group knows which Vermillion is intended. Canoe groups have been known to go to the wrong Vermillion on a scheduled trip, much to the embarrassment of trip leaders.

The Vermillion River offers to the expert canoeist the most respected whitewater rapids in the state. To shoot the chute known as the "Wildcat," it is best to have two paddlers and no gear aboard. To prevent shipping of water and swamping, the bow paddler should kneel behind the front seat, or thwart, to bring up the bow. Once through the rapids, the crew must quickly maneuver to prevent the canoe from being picked up by the strong back eddy that would take the canoe to the rocks. The Vermillion is not all so wild, however. Its rural banks are forested, and in the spring its flowering crab, redbud, and hawthorn blossoms are spectacular. Pine and juniper abound on the 80- to 100-foot-high bluffs, and wild flowers embroider the landscape along the way.

Most canoe trips on the Vermillion River begin at the Pontiac area. The river varies in width from 30 to over 100 feet. The bottom is mostly gravel, and riffle and rapids are numerous. As most of the river flows through private land, permission must be obtained for camping, put-in, and takeout.

The river distance from the dam at Pontiac to Route 23 in Streator is approximately twenty-eight miles, just right for a day's trip if the water level is high enough to take you over the obstructions. There is a private campground where the river crosses Route 23, north of Cornell. In general, launchings as well as takeouts can be made at any of the highway bridges. This is a good rule of thumb when in any unknown stretch of water.

Access in Streator is available for small groups on the southwest side of the bridge, south of Route 18, at the power-house. From here it is seventeen miles to the Lowell bridge, where access is also available. Should you plan to put in or take out at the Lowell bridge, drive off of Route 178 on the side road north of the bridge and park at the end, by the old bridge abutment.

Traveling downstream below the Lowell bridge means navigating the whitewater portion of the Vermillion. Canoe-ing here is restricted to periods of relatively high water, and even then it is for experienced paddlers only. The speed of the current through this section is about ten miles per hour, and hydraulic turbulence may cause waves as high as five feet. The steep gradient of the river leads to the Wildcat chute, the shooting of which was mentioned earlier.

Because water conditions vary on the Class II-rated Wildcat rapids, it is best to approach with caution, scouting it first from the right bank. Should you decide to portage around the Wildcat, take out on the left bank. After the Wildcat you are not out of the woods yet. Cement Dam Rap-ids are next. The Marquette Cement Company dam spans most of the river and must be run via the chute on the right side. Keep as close as possible to the remaining section of the dam and brace for a drop of approximately two feet. At the new level turn sharply to the left, riding the current to bring the stern around and avoid the haphazardly situated underwater rocks.

Note: The takeout is an involved and tricky procedure. On your first visit to the Vermillion it would probably be wise to attach yourself to one of the many Illinois canoe groups that regularly schedule trips to conquer the Wildcat rapids.

The Vermillion offers good fishing for bass, bluegill, bullhead, and carp. The best spots are reported to be in the section below Pontiac near the county line bridge as well as west of Cornell, south of Streator, north of Lowell, and east of Oglesby.

Little Vermillion River

This river offers the sportiest whitewater course in Illinois, according to veteran canoeists. From the vicinity of LaSalle the Little Vermillion drops, tumbles, and roars through a 115-foot drop at an average gradient of seventeen feet per mile. The river contains two dams and five rapids, one of which is Canyon Rapids, rated Class III in difficulty by virtue of its thirteen-foot drop in 300 feet. Even expert kayakers have difficulty conquering Canyon Rapids.

Though it is not within the province of this book to discuss whitewater kayaking, here are directions, should you wish to take a look at the Little Vermillion: For the put-in from I-80, take the first exit west of Utica to Route 351. Drive south to the first crossroad, less than one-half mile away. Turn right (west) on the gravel road and follow it for about one-half mile to another gravel road. Turn right and drive slightly less than two miles north, beyond the interstate highway, again to the first gravel road. Turn right again and drive east for less than one-half mile to the next crossroad. Turn left and continue to the bridge about one-half mile away.

Finding the takeout point is quite involved: Take Route 35 to the south end of LaSalle. At the first intersection south of 1st Street turn right and drive west about 200 feet to the small bridge crossing the railroad tracks. (The Illinois-Michigan Canal is on the left.) Turn left on the bridge and cross both the tracks and canal to the parking lot beyond. The pickup point is on the right bank, about 400 feet away.

Rock River

From Wisconsin the Rock River enters Illinois near Rockton, in Winnebago County, and continues for nearly 150 miles of scenic, gentle canoeing. The river flows through a succession of towns and cities, and cottages are frequently seen along the banks. The Rock is a consistently wide river that averages fifteen feet in depth and offers a good current ranging from one to two miles per hour. It can be canoed throughout all the warm months of the year except in extreme drought, of course.

From Rock River to the Canadian waters, the "good life" is often only a canoe, and a couple.

The gentle beauty of the Rock river can be enjoyed by less than hardy canoeists, who can choose to spend the night at hotels or motels and eat meals at restaurants in the towns along the way. As an example, a weekend trip from Blackhawk Park, south of Rockford near the 15th Street Bridge, to Dixon offers a nonstrenuous weekend trip. Plan to have lunch at Byron, and three to four hours of paddling later you can spend the night at Oregon. The portage at the dam at Oregon is relatively easy. The next day you can paddle the remaining twenty miles to Dixon through the most scenic section of the river. Take time out to climb Castle Rock and to visit historic Grand Detour. Takeout is at the city park at Dixon, a few miles above the dam.

Below Dixon the river reaches its greatest depth—as much as fifty feet in places in the stretch toward Sterling. This part of the river is excellent for canoeing, although it is somewhat less scenic than the section above Dixon.

Below Sterling and Rock Falls the surrounding countryside consists of low farmland. There is a gentle current, numerous small islands, and the river is free of dams until you approach the mouth of the river, where it empties into the Mississippi.

The best fishing in the Rock River is found in the tailwater (water below the dams). Channel catfish, bullhead, crappie, walleye, and carp are the species most frequently caught. The months of late spring and early summer seem to be the best fishing periods.

Along the entire course of the Rock River public launching areas are available—at the Sportsmans Club and the Macktown Forest Preserve at Rockton, at the Lowden State Park and at the Oregon Dam at Oregon, at Lowell Park in Dixon, at the Lawrence Park ramp at Sterling, and at the Prophetstown State Park at Prophetstown. Campsites are available at Lowden State Park, Prophetstown State Park, the Erie Boating Club at Erie, and at Landuit Lake at Joslin.

Should you wish to take an upriver trip to Wisconsin, the short cruise from Rockton to Fort Atkinson is pleasant, although powerboats frequent the area. A mechanical lift maintained by the Janesville Boat Club provides an easy bypass of the Indianford Dam on the way to Lake Koshkonong. This 10,000-acre lake, for the most part less than seven feet in depth, can become quite rough under windy conditions. The area below Fort Atkinson is a prime site of white bass activity during their spawning runs, in early spring.

Des Plaines River

The Des Plaines River flows from northern Lake County through Cook, DuPage, and Will counties. In Will County it joins with the Kankakee to form the Illinois River. The upper portion of the Des Plaines is a narrow, shallow stream, but when it reaches southern Lake and northern Cook counties, it develops some strength. Even though the river meanders through built-up areas, once midstream canoeists are likely to become oblivious to sounds of civilization as they cruise past forested areas interspersed with tilled land and wild fields. Added visual experiences unfold in a profusion of wild flowers, bird life, waterfowl, muskrat colonies, lush growth of water plants in the backoffs, and long vistas framed by overhanging willows.

On the river's southerly course evidence of people and vehicles appear as the canoeist approaches bridges, but they just as quickly disappear upon leaving them. The bridges, which serve as put-in and takeout points, include Grand Avenue at Gurnee (Route 132); Belvidere Road (Route 120); Oak Spring Road and Rockland Road in Libertyville; Town Line Road (Route 60); Half Day Road (Route 22); Deerfield Road; and Lake–Cook Road (Route 68), the gateway to Cook County.

Before leaving Lake County, north of Deerfield Road one sees the Ryerson Conservation Area on the east side of the river. The area represents one of the last remaining examples of mature maple-basswood floodplain forest in the state. The woods have not been extensively grazed or clear-cut and therefore appear much the same as when the settlers arrived. In this unique preserve many species of plants and animals are found, including the blue-spotted salamander and the Brewsters warbler, whose only known nesting location in Illinois is at the south end of the preserve.

The stretch from the Ryerson Conservation Area to Dam 2 is the scene of my boyhood canoeing. As high school students, we purchased a used wood and canvas seventeen-footer at Willow Springs and paddled it about thirty-five miles upstream to camp "House in the Wood" (the present site of the River Trail Nature Center), where we served as counselors. As our days were activity filled and responsibility laden, most of our canoeing was done after taps.

> ... We launched the canoe and floated the calm current in total darkness. There was little concern about danger, as we were expert swimmers and knew every foot of the shoreline. In the middle of the river we just laid back, paddles at rest, drifting with the current, time, and history ... akin to the aboriginal Indians, Marquette, Jolliet, LaSalle, and Tonti, intrepid voyagers who cruised the river in an earlier time. In kinship with these explorer–patriots we listened to the same night sounds ... *

Enhancing the canoeing experiences on this portion of the Des Plaines River is the fact that from Lake–Cook Road at the Potawatomi Woods to 47th Street in Lyons at the Ottowa Trail Woods practically the entire river's course (about thirty miles) weaves through Cook County forest preserves. It also passes two nature centers with exhibits and resident naturalists.

The Forest Preserve District of Cook County, Illinois, comprises 64,750 acres. The preserves are not parks but sanctuaries of native landscape, flora, and fauna. Of the total acreage, eighty percent remains in a wild or semiwild state. Nowhere in the United States is there such a large area of publicly owned landscape as fine and as readily accessible to so many people.

While paddling through the Potawatomi Woods, canoeists can get a feel for the historic past blending with contemporary landscapes. Along the way can be seen the site of an Indian village, an arrowhead chipping site, a remnant of original Illinois prairie, sites of pioneer settlers, and early 20th-century farmlands that today are returning to

---

*John W. Malo, "Love Affair with a River," *Outdoor Illinois*, May 1977.

their original state of wildness. Welcome, on a hot summer day, are the huge cottonwoods and weeping willows that cascade over the river. The towering hard maples, oak, and hickory trees show their beauty best in the autumn.

This stretch of the Des Plaines offers leisurely and contemplative paddling. And inland from the river, especially off the well-trod paths, there is opportunity for experiencing miles and miles of silence. This haven of water and wood was the scene of many of the outdoor adventures recorded in my *Tranquil Trails,* a nature diary.*

This route will take you past four dams. The movement of the water over the dams causes a considerable undertow in this area, so portaging is recommended, particularly in light of the fact that a few fatalities have occurred here. Accesses are plentiful and convenient all along the route, and several of the dams have boat rollers, which can be used for easy portaging.

Farther downstream, the river is heavily used by local canoe-owning families, especially in the Willow Springs, Lemont, Lockport, and Joliet areas. The proximity to the river enables the locals to be afloat without much preparation or extensive car travel. They paddle, practice techniques, and picnic, and lovers cruise by moonlight.

A FAR-FAMED DES PLAINES RIVER EVENT.   The Des Plaines River from Libertyville, Illinois, to Dam 2 sees a lot of canoeing action every year on the last Sunday in May. This is the site of the nation's largest single canoe race over a twenty-mile course.

The Illinois Paddling Council (IPC) sponsors the Annual Des Plaines River Canoe Marathon. The marathon exemplifies what can be accomplished by a closely knit group with excellent leadership. The 20th annual marathon, held in 1977, drew 840 craft. Men and women of all ages had twenty-two events to choose from.

---

*John W. Malo, *Tranquil Trails* (Matteson, Ill.: Great Lakes Living Press, 1977).

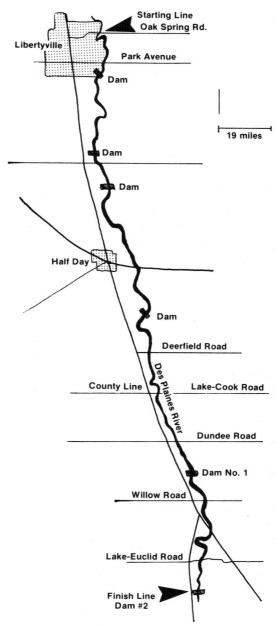

Map of the Annual Des Plaines Canoe Marathon.

Over the years the marathon has offered an excellent example of the nonpolluting, nondisturbing nature of the canoe as a watercraft. After the hundreds upon hundreds of craft and participants finish the race, an inspection of the entire course indicates no evidence that such a profusion of craft, men, women, and children had used the river.

The annual marathon is but one event sponsored by the IPC. They are also in the forefront of stream clean-up campaigns, instructional classes, national competition, canoe trail mapping, and legislation. Above all, the IPC realizes that our water heritage must be zealously guarded by an ongoing and vigorous program of education.

DuPage River (East Branch)

Once highly polluted, the water quality of the DuPage is steadily improving. Its location, not far from the Chicago metropolitan area, offers relaxing cruising that is but a short distance away from the tumult and hubbub of the city.

A leisurely trip of about eighteen miles begins at Plainfield and ends at the Channahon locks and dam. Much of the route is less than spectacular because of built-up areas and highway noises, and there is a stretch of dead water where the river approaches Channahon. As in all rivers, however, there are natural landscapes, overhanging foliage, woodlands, and fields that loom and surprise canoeists as they round the river bends.

The put-in is reached by taking Route 55 (Stevenson Expressway) to the Route 126 exit near Plainfield. Continue southwesterly to Plainfield until it crosses Route 30. Immediately after, without going as far as the bridge, park on the west shoulder of the road, unload, and carry the gear and canoe down the ditch. The put-in is at the state-owned right-of-way below the bridge. The takeout point is at Channahon State Park, between the locks and the dam.

DuPage River (West Branch)

This is smallmouth bass water, ideal for canoeists who wish to fish along the way. Local fishers say, in testimonial to the effectiveness of live crayfish as bait, that every soft-shelled crayfish means a decoyed smallmouth. Drift the crayfish in the shallow riffles late in the evening hours and in the deep holes during the day.

Northwest of Wheaton the west branch offers its best canoeing during the high water periods, which occur mostly in the spring. The put-in is at Route 64 (North Avenue) between Fair Oaks and Prince Crossing roads. Cruise the winding stream south through Spring Lake Preserve and DuPage Park, past Alternate Route 30 (Roosevelt Road) near West Chicago, and then through pastoral scenery to the park and dam at Warrenville. A portage takeout is on the right bank, after which the cruise can continue for twelve more miles to McDowell Woods. Should you wish to continue, there is an easy portage here on the left. After another fifteen miles or so you will be in Naperville. The takeout is at the Route 65 bridge.

Big Muddy River

This river, deep in southwest Illinois, is best enjoyed by skipping the upper reaches and its tributaries because of their difficult canoeing conditions—log jams, narrow width, overgrown shorelines, and so on. The Big Muddy becomes an interesting and challenging course from the Route 51 bridge put-in to its confluence with the Mississippi River. It is a recommended two-day trip for those who enjoy natural beauty or those who are serious students of geology and the biotic world.

There is also access at the city park in Murphysboro, which is about forty-one miles from the mouth of the river. Below the town the quality of the stream improves considerably, widening from 50 to 150 feet and averaging four feet in depth. As it heads first west and then south, the river runs through the Shawnee National Forest. The trees on the riverbanks in this area consist of bottomland hardwood species. With luck, here you will catch sight of the rare pileated woodpecker. Deer abound, but so do rattlesnakes, cottonmouth moccasins, and copperheads, so extreme care must be taken when camping out at night. A tent with a built-in floor is a must. There is a campsite in the Little Grand Canyon, which comprises one of the few remaining wild areas in Illinois.

An access point is located one-fourth mile east of Sand Ridge at a county bridge. Another is east of Route 3 on Johns Spur Road, and a third is at Rattlesnake Ferry, east of Grand Tower. Plan to leave the river at the Route 3 bridge, before it empties into the Mississippi River. Should you wish to include the big river in your itinerary, this would involve paddling upstream on the Mississippi to Grand Tower or downstream several miles to Cape Girardeau. Scenic areas, many with quaint and folksy names, include Abneyville, Swallow Bluffs, Little Grand Canyon, Horseshoe Bluff, and Sinner's Harbor (one wonders about the origin of this last name.)

Cache River

The Cache River was named by Pere Mermet in 1702, when he accompanied the French explorer Jucheceau St. Denis overland from the Mississippi River to the French fur post of Va Bache. Bache was on the Ohio River at the mouth of a creek, and as they approached it, the feeder creek was concealed beneath a massive log jam and other floating debris. Father Mermet is reported to have said, "Cette Crique ist Cache," or "This creek is hidden."

The Cache River flows from a point near Cobden, the "Home of the Apple Knockers," in Union County. It meanders in a generally southerly direction, touching four counties before reaching its terminus at the Ohio River. The upper part of the Cache, above Hollis Spur in Johnson County, is not prime canoeing water because of its shallowness, muddy banks, poisonous snakes, and lack of access, food supplies, and drinking water. On the other hand, for intrepid canoests this section promises an ancient Indian campsite on Boss Island, fossil tree specimens, a cypress swamp, some virgin woods, and 300-foot-high cliffs—all difficult to reach because of swamps, dense jungle growth, and rocky footing.

The take-in recommended for most canoeists is at the bridge between Belknap and Karnak. In four to five hours of interesting paddling time you will be at the bridge south of Perks. The area was once a major lumbering center, and after the lowland trees were harvested, the swampy land was drained for farming. Many of the early farmers were slaves who had come north and settled in small communities called "perks." Later, the town of Perks was established and named for these small settlements.

There is a bridge access on the blacktop road that leads west from the town of Mounds to Routes 3 and 127. You can get off the highway here in dry weather and drive fairly close to the river on the west side south of the bridge for takeout. The bridges on Route 31 and 51 are to be avoided.

While in this area of southern Illinois, allow sufficient time for visits to the Ozark-like scenery of the Horseshoe Lake Conservation Area, the Pine Hills Conservation Area, and the Shawnee National Forest.

Little Wabash River

Discount any section of this stream north of Carmi. The portion of the river that is canoeable is a stretch of about twenty-five miles between Carmi (put in at Route 1) and New Haven, just before the river's confluence with the

Wabash River. The cruise is through rural areas with few roads and bridges. There are good camping areas on private land, and, therefore, permission must be obtained from landowners.

The river is scenic and can be traveled by canoe almost anytime of the year. Bedrock outcroppings among the forested banks offer interesting shorelines. Fishing is good in this little-traveled stretch of the river. Takeout is at New Haven (Route 141).

Wabash River

Paddle the Wabash River and take out on the Illinois side near Mount Carmel. Visit Beall Woods, a vestige of original Illinois bottomland, where the oldest Shumard oak in the United States stands in a 625-acre tract of virgin trees, some rising 150 feet. The tall, bleached, dead bottomland trees are the favorite haunt of the pileated woodpecker, a species distinguished by its habit of drilling squarish, oblong holes. Chances are you will hear more often than see this rare bird. This stretch of the Wabash serves as part of the Illinois–Indiana border and is discussed in the next chapter, "Adventure Trails of Indiana."

Sangamon River

The canoeist in Illinois can retrace Abraham Lincoln's flatboat cruise that took him to Salem, from where he went on to immortality. The shoreline along the Lincoln Heritage Canoe Trail down the Sangamon retains to this day some of the character it had in Lincoln's day. The Sangamon was the first stream in Illinois to be dedicated as a canoe trail, and its establishment as such served to highlight the historical and recreational potential of the river.

The upper portion of the Sangamon is not considered to be suitable for canoeing because of the numerous natural and man-made obstructions. The historic stretch that is paddled quite heavily runs from the Lincoln Trail Homestead State Park to New Salem State Park.

The put-in is at the state park on Route 36, west of Decatur, where there are excellent facilities—rest rooms, picnic tables, drinking water, and a launching site. Here the river has a good current, ranges in depth from one foot over riffles to twelve feet in some pools, and varies in width from 60 to 325 feet. Above Springfield the bottom is predominantly sand and gravel; below, it is mostly muddy. The industrial influence of Decatur shows in the quality of the water; it is discolored, silted, and algae-ridden, particularly in the warm months.

There is a campsite with launching on the northeast side of the Buckhart Bridge. Being the property of Buckhart Sand & Gravel Co., permission for its use must be obtained at the company's office. From this point it is a few miles to the Riverton Riverside Park, which has facilities available between May 20 and October 1. If you launch here, notify the Riverton Village Hall in advance. The parking lot is at the top of the hill.

Approaching the north edge of Springfield, one finds Carpenter Park,* just off Route 66, which has an excellent camping area and parking lot. In the town proper a low dam requires an easy portage. At high water levels the dam is completely covered, so portaging is unnecessary. The next available campsite is at Salisbury Bridge. This is a wilderness canoe base located on the right side of the river, about 100 yards below the bridge.

After a long day's paddle from Springfield, you will reach New Salem State Park. Take out at the old grist mill on Route 97. There is a parking lot nearby as well as rest rooms, a camping supply store, and restaurants open throughout the year. And by all means plan to stay long enough to visit and absorb the haunts of Lincoln's early manhood.

---

*Notice of intent to use the camping area should be sent to Springfield Park District, Bunn Park Pavilion, Springfield, Illinois.

Kankakee River

In 1679 LaSalle cruised the Kankakee from its source in Indiana to its confluence with the Illinois River. The 20th-century canoeist can paddle the same course and, in a stop-over hike, enjoy the same deep ravines, view the waterfowl in the backwaters, and perhaps catch a walleye. The Kankakee is one of the few rivers in Illinois that supports this delectable fish.

Two good accesses with adequate parking are just across the stateline in Indiana—at the Route 41 bridge and at the LaSalle State Fish and Game Area. East of here the marshy river valley offers the possibility of sighting numerous sandhill cranes that flock to the area. Bird-watchers come long distances to observe this crane, much like the great blue heron, during its recurring visits.

On its approach to Momence the river flows over eroded Silurian limestone to produce an interesting series of small rapids and riffles that is an exciting experience for beginning canoeists. The town offers accesses at Island Park and Aroma Park off Route 17. About two miles south of Route 17 the road runs near the river, making for easy access.

Downstream from Momence all the way to Kankakee, the river is lined with a profusion of riverside vacation homes, fishing shacks, and permanent habitations. Many of the limestone ledges are followed by deep pools, some as much as eighteen feet deep, and with the high water and strong current from spring rain runoff, the Kankakee can become quite feisty.

Access at Kankakee is at Alpine Park, upstream of the bridge. Another is one block west of the Route 45 bridge; put in on the right bank. At the dam in town, portage before reaching the railroad bridge, on the north side of the river, just below the first bridge. The carry is west along the river, past the dam to the Route 45 bridge where you cross it to the south side of the river. Then you must go west again behind a small commercial area to the park access.

About eight miles of paddling takes you to the Kankakee River State Park. The shoreline offers many pleasing sights: impressive rock outcrops, wooded islands, a rock wall of up to twenty-five feet in height, farmland and meadows, and eye-appealing hilltop residences.

The takeout is at the public landing in Kankakee River State Park. The park is open all year and offers a fine campground as well as facilities essential to the needs of the canoeist. There is a deep ravine just north of the park that offers a nice hike—a welcome respite from paddling.

Saline River

The Saline runs through hilly land. To the canoeist willing to beach the canoe and climb a riverside hilltop prominence, the river offers spectacular views, especially the autumnal coloration of the oaks, hickories, and smaller trees. At the town of Equality stands the site of an early French stockade built about 1869 and farther downstream, the Ghost Indian Salt Springs, the Indians' source of salt. Beyond that the Saline empties into the Ohio River.

The stretch of river from Equality to Saline Landing provides nice, easy canoeing between high riverbanks. Access is from the county road bridge just south of town. Load up on supplies before leaving Equality, as this is the last chance to get drinking water, food, and other supplies. Mastodon bones have been found at nearby Half-Moon Lick, evidence of the use of salt by prehistoric animals.

Campsites are plentiful, and because of the remoteness of the area, it is an excellent place to be alone and to commune with the flora and fauna of the region. The water level is consistently deep enough to float a canoe; in fact, during most of the year the depth is from four to eight feet. The riverbed is rock, with extensive areas of sand, gravel, and silt.

You can shorten your paddling time by about two hours by substituting the put-in at Equality for the one at the

Route 1 bridge. The water here is reddish in color, but it clears downstream.

Around 1800 this part of Illinois was heavily populated. There were numerous bridges across the Saline, indicating that there was an extensive transportation system. Saline Mines in southeastern Gallatin County was a major government outpost in the wilderness and was located on the first road through Illinois. The tax on salt mined in the area represented a main source of revenue for the state in its early years.

Much of the Saline's course lies within the Shawnee National Forest, which naturally enhances its shorelines. Toward the terminus of the river the water becomes quite salty and gradually changes to a chalky white, but these characteristics do not adversely affect the fishing for bluegill, crappie, or channel catfish. A few more hours of paddling will take you to the Saline Mines Road, where evidence of the nearness of the Ohio River such as floating debris and oil wastes begin to appear. There is no takeout at Saline Mines; you must go to Saline Landing, just before the river empties into the Ohio. You can also go to the Ohio by staying to the right of the island and heading toward the old pier called Seller's Landing. Downstream on the Ohio, about four hours' paddling away, is Cave-in-Rock State Park, a place with an exciting history of harboring pirates who robbed and murdered river-traveling pioneers.

Spoon River

Spoon River Anthology immortalized its author, Edgar Lee Masters, who drew characterizations from the people of the village. Here are a few characteristics of the river. This is a good stream for those who enjoy a little wildness in their trips. The Spoon is more untamed than most Illinois rivers, as few commercial facilities crowd its shorelines.

The most scenic part of the river is the upper half, which abounds in thick underbrush, poison ivy, log jams, high-velocity currents, and variable water levels. A good point of access for recreational paddling is at the Gelvin Bridge on the Stark–Peoria County Line Road. The road is three-fourths of a mile north of the Spoon River Bridge on Route 78, north of Laura. The bridge at Elmore is another access point, and it also offers a suitable place for an overnight camp.

Downstream a few miles, in Dahinda, there is a small store where supplies may be obtained. It is an easy paddle from this place to the historic covered Wolf Bridge, one of the few such bridges in the state. The bridge site is an excellent place to camp, rest, or fish.

Camping is permitted in the city park on the riverbank at London Mills, where supplies can be replenished. About ten miles away is Ellisville, the site of the Creve Coeur Council Scout Camp and Canoe Base, which is reached just upstream on Cedar Creek.

The only dam is at Bernadotte, which under normal water conditions requires a portage. When the water is high and the current is running fast, takeout should be well above the dam to keep from being swept over. Bernadotte dates back to the era of the steamboat and is an interesting place to visit and converse with the local residents. Farmers and townsfolk in western Illinois are reputed for their friendliness and their willingness to cooperate with canoeists and other outdoor enthusiasts.

A takeout here should be considered, since it is about forty miles to Havana on the Illinois River, where the canoeist must deal with open water, speedboaters, and wakes of cruisers and bargetows.

INFORMATION SOURCES

"Illinois Canoeing Guide" is available from the Illinois Department of Conservation, Springfield, Illinois 62706 (Free).
Illinois Paddling Council, 2316 Prospect Avenue, Evanston, Illinois 60201, has pamphlets available.
This is a nonprofit association representing Illinois

canoeists and canoe clubs. Its tenets include the preservation of wild rivers and their natural environment,
arresting and reversing the deterioration of streams,
speaking on behalf of canoeists in matters of conservation, serving as a source of information to midwestern
canoers and kayakers, and making known to the general public the rich canoeing heritage of the state and
the Midwest in general. The Council sponsors mara-
thons, statewide racing, and river clean-up campaigns,
and it issues many canoe-oriented publications for sale.
There are many other Council-sponsored activities and
advantages.

Chicagoland Canoe Base is owned by Ralph Frese, 4019 N.
Narragansett Avenue, Chicago, Illinois 60634, (312)
770-1489.

Ralph's enterprise is touted, with justification, as
"the most unusual canoe shop in the U.S." It has a complete line of rentals, sales, custom-made craft, acces-
sories, equipment, publications, and so on. His creation,
the twenty-foot early Algonquin-style simulated birchbark canoe, has been used extensively in pageants and
historical reenactments. The Base is a mecca for both
local and faraway canoeists. Between multitudinous
chores, Ralph ("Mr. Canoe") expounds on canoeing history, trails, and techniques, and there is always a yarn
or ancedote about canoeing.

Illinois Country Outdoor Guides, by Phil Vierling, 4400 N.
Merrimac Avenue, Chicago, Illinois 60630.

This is a series of canoe trail guides, unsurpassed
anywhere for their detail. The author is a high school
science teacher, active canoe trip leader, and the car-
tographer of the Illinois Paddling Council. Phil has
mapped many Illinois rivers, including information on
how to get to them via highway routes, put-in and takeout options, and car shuttle details. As for the waters
themselves, every mile is completely noted as to the
conditions and character of the river and its shoreline.

The four low-priced booklets are titled "Des Plaines River"; "Fox, Mazon, Vermillion and Little Vermillion Rivers"; "DuPage, Kankakee, Aux Sable and Des Plaines Rivers"; and "Loop Hiking Trail to the Chicago Portage National Historic Site."

Snarr's Paddling Service, 2316 Prospect Avenue, Evanston, Illinois 60201.

Jack and Lynn Snarr, and their two children, also canoeists, are dedicated to all aspects of canoeing and kayaking. Jack, an associate professor of physiology and associate dean for student affairs at the Northwestern University Medical School in Chicago, paddles ten miles down Lake Michigan from his home in Evanston to the Chicago campus. From May to October he averages two round trips a week via the water route. Jack teaches paddling techniques at Patten Gym pool on the Evanston campus, serves on citizens' groups related to water pollution and land use, and is past president of the U.S. Canoe Association. Lynn Snarr is the editor of the Illinois Paddling Council *Newsletter* and is an authority on how to take children canoeing with safety. She outlines a gradation of skills to be mastered, depending on the child's age, strength, and ability.

"Lincoln Heritage Trail" is available from the Department of Economic Development, 222 S. College Street, Springfield, Illinois 62701.

American Youth Hostels, 3712 N. Clark Street, Chicago, Illinois 60613, organizes cruising trips, primarily for nonfamily persons. Canoes and some provisions are furnished.

Illini Downstreamers organizes family canoeing with the emphasis on environment and safety. Contact Leo Krusak, 444 Main Street, Glen Ellyn, Illinois 60137.

Keepataw Canoe Club has monthly cruising trips. Contact Don Muggenberg, 9 Pfiffer Lane, Lemont, Illinois 60439.

Other active groups include the Prairie Club and Lincoln Park Boat Club.

3
Adventure Trails of Indiana

The topography of Indiana is characterized by flat plains and prairie, fertile farmland for grain and stock, and limestone quarries and coal mines. The state is bordered on the south by the Ohio River, and part of its western boundary with Illinois is formed by the Wabash River.

Miami Indians were the earliest inhabitants of the region, as first noted by Father Druilettes in 1658. When the French and English explorers came into the area, groups of Potawatomi, Weas, and other tribes were also in evidence.

LaSalle and Hennepin passed through the region on their way to the Mississippi River in 1679. Another early missionary, Father Allouez, established a mission at St. Joseph, close to the present site of Notre Dame University.

The French established the first permanent white settlement in 1731 at Vincennes; no other was made until after the War of Independence. Kekionga (Fort Wayne) and Ouiatenon (LaFayette) were established around 1819. Also, nine struggling settlements were precariously established along the Wabash River while much of the land was still in the Indians' hands.

Indiana Canoe Trails

Canoeing in Indiana has risen steadily in popularity in recent years. Residents and visitors alike have discovered the potential of secluded rivers and streams to provide a respite from the pressures of overcrowded modern life. Family and club groups, scout troops, and canoe clubs can choose from many trips in the state.

Wabash River

The Indians named this beautiful river "Wabash," which translates to "water over white stones." Famed in song and history, the Wabash is the longest river in Indiana. From the Ohio state line, it flows westward across the upper portion of Indiana through rich farmlands of corn and wheat, then turns southwesterly toward Illinois and flows south through tobacco-growing country to its terminus at the Ohio River.

Numerous access points are spaced along the river's entire course, allowing for many trips of varying lengths. Fed first by the Salamonie and the Mississinewa Rivers, the Wabash picks up more volume from the Eel and Tippecanoe Rivers and finally from the White River, which drains the southern portion of the state. The Wabash empties into the Ohio.

On the bends of the lower Wabash the history of Indiana is revealed. The mellow old city, of Vincennes in Knox County, established in 1705, was the first settlement in the state. Terre Haute and as many as eight other settlements burgeoned soon after, indicating that in Indiana, too, most early settlements originated on watercourses and with the canoe playing a substantial role in their development.

Downriver, New Harmony was founded in 1815 by the Rappites, a communal religious sect of German settlers.

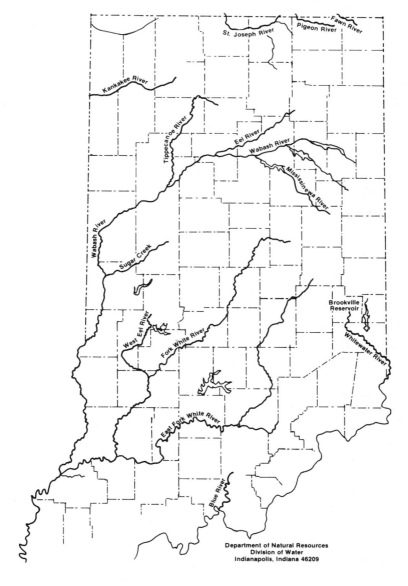

The most popular canoe trails in Indiana.
(Department of Natural Resources, Division of Water, Indianapolis, Indiana, 46209)

Table 3-1. Indiana River Data.

Stream	Location	Portion most Suitable for Canoeing	Approximate Stream Mileage	Number of Known Portages
Blue River	Central	Freeport Dam to Columbus	45 miles	1
Blue River	South Central	Fredricksburg to Ohio River	55 miles	4
Eel River	Northeast	South Whitley to Logansport	60 miles	7
Eel River	West Central	Reelsville to Worthington	50 miles	0
Fawn River	Northeast	From Crooked Creek at Snow Lake to Michigan State Line	20 miles	3
Kankakee River	Northwest	From Kankakee State Game Preserve to Illinois State Line	55 miles	0
Mississinewa River	East Central	From Eaton to Peru	60 miles	7
Muscatatuck River	Southeast	North of Austin to Sparksville	30 miles	0
Pigeon River	Northeast	From Dam at Mongo to Michigan State Line	20 miles	4
St. Joseph River	North Central	From Bristol West to Michigan State Line	35 miles	4
Sugar Creek	Northwest	From Darlington to Montezuma	45 miles	4
Tippecanoe River	North	From Rochester to Lafayette	75 miles	2
Wabash River	Northeast to Southwest	From Bluffton to Ohio River	360 miles	3
White River (East Fork)	South Central to Southwest	From Columbus to Mt. Carmel, Illinois	175 miles	4
White River (West Fork)	Central to Southwest	West edge of Anderson to Mt. Carmel, Illinois	210 miles	6
Whitewater River	East Central	Connersville to Ohio River	55 miles	1

Many of the original stone buildings, such as the Old Rappite Fort and the Community House, still remain.

The 451-mile Wabash River, from the Ohio state line to its terminus at the Ohio River, is best divided into three stretches for canoeing purposes. They are from the state line to Lafayette, Lafayette to Hutsonville (on the Illinois side), and Hutsonville to the Ohio River. The following access points represent supply points for food, water, and general river information.

For good water conditions and access points, the first stretch is probably best traveled from Markel (Route 3) to Andrews, 18.6 miles; from Andrews to Wabash, 14.2 miles; from Wabash to Peru, 14.6 miles; from Peru to Logansport, 18 miles; from Logansport to Delphi, 23.8 miles; and from Delphi to the Main Street bridge at Lafayette, 14.2 miles.

The second stretch includes Lafayette to Attica, 23.9 miles; Attica to Covington, 16.7 miles; Covington to Perrysville, 6.8 miles; Perrysville to Montezuma, 24.4 miles; Montezuma to Clinton, 10 miles; Clinton to Terre Haute, 15.9 miles; and Terre Haute to Hutsonville, Illinois, 40.7 miles.

The final stretch of the Wabash River is from Hutsonville, Illinois, to Merom, Indiana, 7.2 miles; Merom to Russelville, Illinois, 25 miles; Russelville to Vincennes, Indiana, 12.7 miles; Vincennes, Indiana, to St. Francisville, Illinois, 12.3 miles; St. Francisville to Mt. Carmel, Illinois, 21 miles; Mt. Carmel to Crawleyville, Indiana, 9.5 miles; Crawleyville to Grayville, Illinois, 20.6 miles; Grayville to New Harmony, Indiana, 9.8 miles; New Harmony to Maunee, Illinois, 10.2 miles; and Maunee to the Ohio River, 34.5 miles. Throughout the entire 451-mile course, the Wabash drops but 3.4 feet, presenting no major problem.

Today the Wabash can still evoke the same feelings that inspired Paul Dresser's "On the Banks of the Wabash":

> Oh, the moonlight's fair tonight along the Wabash,
> From the field there comes the breath of new-mown hay
> Thro' the sycamores the candelights are gleaming,
> On the banks of the Wabash far away.

Tippecanoe River

The Tippecanoe River, with five access points, flows for approximately 150 miles with a moderate drop that contributes to a peaceful cruise to its juncture with the Wabash. The canoe trail leads through Tippecanoe River State Park (2,744 acres), and below Winamac the Norway Dam backs up the water to form Lake Shafer, a good place to fish for bass, bluegill, and catfish.

Youngsters, properly protected, try out their muscle on a calm Lake Shafer.
(Bob O'Reilly Photography, Fort Wayne, Indiana)

The Tippecanoe trip is probably best begun at the access near Rochester (Route 31). Farther downstream there are other access points at intervals as follows: Rochester to Leiteus Ford, 15 miles; Leiteus Ford to Monterey, 7.7 miles; Monterey to Tippecanoe State Park to Winamac, 16 miles; Winamac to Lake Shafer with a portage at Norway dam, then to the Monticello takeout, 31.5 miles. The average fall per mile over the above course is about two feet, indicating few navigation problems. Supplies, food, water, and so on are available at the access points.

Sugar Creek

This water course is famed for its visual impact and its fast-dropping water (average fall per mile is five feet). It is also famed for its spectacular course through gorges that take the canoeist through two of Indiana's finest state parks—Shades and Turkey Run.

For more time to enjoy the parks, it is best to put in below the dam at Crawfordsville; from there it is sixteen miles to Shades State Park. This haven of natural beauty offers fishing in Sugar Creek and hiking over interesting trails that wind through dense woods and deep ravines. This area preserves for all posterity the natural beauty of primitive Indiana.

It is eleven miles from Shades to Turkey Run State Park. The setting is a geological treat; the work of natural forces in a prehistoric age has resulted in deep, cool, rock-walled canyons and gorges as Sugar Creek twists through solid rock. There are large tracts of virgin wood, thirteen miles of foot trails, and twenty miles of bridle paths. Should you wish to stop over, keep in mind that the Turkey Run Inn is so popular that reservations are made a year in advance.

From the park to the Wabash River is 12.5 miles, and it is 4.7 miles farther to the Route 36 takeout at the town of Montezuma.

Mississinewa River

This river, flowing for 110 miles from the Ohio state line, falls 3.3 feet per mile and eventually spills into the Wabash. Frances Slocum State Forest is located along its shores, and there is fishing in the impoundments from the dams near Matthews and Marion.

The portion of the stream from Eaton (near Route 3) to Peru is deemed most favorable for canoeing. To help you plan your cruising program, whether an overnighter or a one-day trip, the mileages between access and supply points are noted here: Eaton to Matthews, 12.1 miles; Matthews to Gas City, 11.7 miles; Gas City to Marion, 7.2 miles; Marion to Redbridge (this stretch is the Mississinewa Reservoir), 25.7 miles; and Redbridge to the Wabash River at the town of Peru, approximately 12 miles, completes the trip.

Whitewater River

The Whitewater River is aptly named, for it is the fastest flowing stream in Indiana, and as such it should be attempted only by skilled canoeists. Its east and west forks combine at Brookville to create a powerful volume of water. With its rock and log obstructions, it is a challenge to the skills of the best canoeist. The Whitewater races to the Ohio River, the mother that tempers its flow.

The best portion of the Whitewater River is known to be from the Laurel Dam to the Ohio River. Distances include Laurel to Metamora (Route 52), 5.8 miles; Metamora to Brookville, 11.2 miles; Brookville to Cedar Grove bridge (Route 1), 8.5 miles; Cedar Grove to Harrison, Ohio, 12.3 miles; Harrison to Elizabethtown, Ohio, 9.1 miles; Elizabethtown to the Ohio River, 6.2 miles; and takeout at Lawrenceburg, Indiana, 2.3 miles. The total mileage is 68.6, with a total fall in the river of 339 feet. This is an average fall of 2.7 feet per mile.

East Fork of the White River

The Driftwood and the Flat Rock rivers combine at Columbus to form the East Fork of the White River. As it flows southward, a dam backs up the water into a quiet fishing area below Azalia. Nearby at Bedford are limestone quarries from which comes the famous Bedford stone for the world's finest buildings. Then comes a unique experience for canoeists—cruising under covered bridges near Brownstown and New Medora. Time your visit to coincide with the nearby Brown County Covered Bridge Festival, which is held annually, and you will enjoy many facets of Americana.

A tourist takes time to appreciate and photograph the Brown County Covered Bridge.

A suggested first access and supply point is below the dam at Columbus. Following access points, in order, are: Azalia, about 12 miles away; the dam north of Seymour, 11.7 miles; the covered bridge near Brownstown, 17.4 miles; the covered bridge near Medora, 10.6 miles; and to Sparksville, 12.9 miles.

The second portion of the East Fork is characterized by a snaky and interesting course with relatively flat water. From Sparksville, the access and supply points follow in this order: to Tunnelton, 13.2 miles; to Lawrenceport, 4.5 miles; to the highway bridge on Route 50 near Bedford, 12.1 miles; Route 50 to the dam at Williams, 15 miles; to Shoals, 23.2 miles; to Hindustan Falls, 13.4 miles; to the Route 231 highway bridge near Haysville, 15 miles; to the junction with the West Fork, about 25 miles; and to the Route 61 bridge near Petersburg, 6 miles. At this point you will be on the White River proper, with Hazelton 27 miles away and Mt. Carmel, Illinois, on the Wabash, 19 miles farther.

The entire course of the East Fork of the White River

(140 miles) averages a drop of less than three feet per mile and offers a leisurely, safe journey.

West Fork of the White River

As the upper reaches of the West Fork from Perkinsville to Martinsville are harnessed by eight dams requiring portages, it is recommended to begin the cruise at Paragon and go from there to the river's confluence with the East Fork, near Petersburg.

Access is from the bridge south of Paragon (Route 67). Go from there to the bridge at Gosport (6.8 miles), then to McCormick's Creek State Park (9.8 miles). Here you may wish to try your hand at paddling up McCormick's Creek, which rushes, falls, and cuts its way through a limestone canyon. Take a break from paddling to enjoy the park: hike the trails to explore the beech woods, pine forests, ravines, sinkholes, deep stone gullies, and abandoned quarry. The park offers excellent housing accommodations, ranging from the Canyon Inn to family housekeeping and camper cabins.

From here it is 15.8 miles to the bridge at Freedom; to Route 157 at Worthington, 14.2 miles; to Route 54 at Bloomfield, 9.7 miles; to Route 58 near Elnora, 22.3 miles; to Route 358 at Edwardsport, 20.6 miles, and from Edwardsport to the junction with the East Fork of the White River, approximately 28 miles. To Mt. Carmel, Illinois, on the Wabash, it is about 50 miles.

Eel Rivers

Note. There are two Eel rivers in Indiana. They are unrelated and located in different parts of the state. They can be distinguished by their sources and their confluences with other rivers—one with the Wabash and one with the White.

The Eel River in the northeastern sector of the state flows through Whitley, Wabash, Miami, Tippecanoe, and Cass

The quiet waters above dams set the scene for relaxed family cruising.

counties and then empties into the Wabash River. In the best canoeing portion of the river (approximately 65 miles), from South Whitley to the Wabash River, there are eight carryovers. The various access and supply points break down this way: from South Whitley to Collamer Dam, 2.6 miles; to Liberty Hills Dam, 6.2 miles; to North Manchester Dam, 6 miles; to Laketon, 4.3 miles; to Roann, 8.5 miles; to Denver, 14.4 miles; and to the Wabash River, 21.1 miles. The average fall per mile on this stretch of the Eel River is 2.7 feet.

The other Eel River in Indiana is located in the west central portion of the state. It flows through Putnam, Clay, Owen, and Greene counties. In Greene County it empties into the White River.

This river offers smooth cruising without man-made obstructions along its course of fifty-six miles. The put-in is from Route 40 at Manhattan. After 5.6 miles there is the junction with Mill Creek, which is dammed above to form

Cataract Lake. From the Mill Creek junction to Bowling Green, is 13.3 miles, and from Bowling Green to Worthington and the confluence with the White River is 37.5 miles. In addition to the above-mentioned accesses, there are two roadside put-ins in Clay County and one in southeast Owen County.

Pigeon River

This stream in northeast Indiana from Mongo to the Michigan state line* is a twenty-mile cruise with four well-defined portages. There are adequate camp areas, access points, and places of interest. Features include Mongo Mill Pond; Horseshoe and Goose Neck bends in the river; dams at Mongo, Nasby, and Ontario; and a tamarack marsh, which gives the water its light brown hue, the color of tea.

Spring is the time to float this river, for the canoeist will be treated to meadows in bloom and trillium covering the banks and fields in milky white panoramas for miles along the way. The first bird migrants will also enliven the cruise during this season.

Little Pigeon River

This river lies in the extreme southwestern part of the state and is not related to the Pigeon River in the northeast. When he was eight years old, Abraham Lincoln lived in Gentryville (Route 231) in Spencer County. The Little Pigeon River flows gently by this town, and Lincoln buffs will probably wish to wet their feet or paddles in a creek whose banks and sandy bottom knew the bare feet of Abe.

---

*Complete information on water conditions and canoe rental is available at the Pigeon River State Fish and Game headquarters, located approximately one-half mile east of Mongo on Route 3, between U.S. 20 on the south and State Route 120 on the north. Detailed information on other activities is available from the area manager, R.R. 2, Howe, Indiana 46526.

Elkhart River

The Elkhart* ends at the city of the same name. The Indians noted that one of the river's islands resembled an elk's head, hence the name Elkhart. There are colonies of Amish farmers along some stretches of the river, and you can observe their interesting customs and life-style, dedicated to the simple, nonmechanized life. The Amish disdain modern conveniences, luxuries, and materialism in general.

The Elkhart rises in northern Indiana and joins the St. Joseph at the town of Elkhart. In its upper reaches the river is shallow and slow moving, bordered on either side by marshland that comprises the largest single area of remaining wetland in the state. Waterfowl thrive in this watery expanse that offers food, cover, and nesting havens.

There are some log and vegetation obstructions in the upper reaches, which complicate cruising during high water periods. In the farming sections one should be watchful for barbed wire fencing strung across the river.

The first trip, about twelve miles, is from the put-in point at the Route 13 bridge, just south of Millersburg, to the takeout at the Route 40 bridge in Waterford Mills. About two miles below the put-in there is an old canal, originally built in conjunction with a dam for power generation. Today the dam is gone, but if you bear right the canal offers a half-hour shortcut. The canal later rejoins the river at the location of a small dam, a portage is then necessary on the right. The takeout is farther downstream, at Waterford Mills, as indicated earlier. Food, supplies, and water must be carried, all of which are available at Millersburg, Waterford Mills, Goshen, and Elkhart.

The trip from Waterford Mills to Oxbow Park is a five-hour paddle. Camping is available at Oxbow Park. South of

---

*Information on river conditions, campsites, canoe rentals, and so on is available from Elkhart County Park Department and the Goshen Park Department.

Carrying over a log obstruction represents another canoe tripping technique to be learned.

Goshen is Goshen Pond. At its upper end there are two channels, a canal on the right and the river on the left, which you follow to the dam. Portage is on the right side. The river takes you right through the center of Goshen. Four miles down is Oxbow Park, on the left. Should you wish to terminate the trip here, there is access to Route 33 for pickup.

Most canoe trippers wish to see the confluence of the Elkhart and St. Joseph rivers, which is just three hours away. At the end of the short cruise to Island Park and before the confluence there is a dam, which is portaged on the left. Access is convenient at Sycamore Street, which leads to Route 33.

Flatrock River

This waterway, which flows for about 88 miles, was once lined with various mills that served the Hoosier settlers. The numerous water-powered mills, utilizing the large, flat, grinding rocks that ground the farmers' grain, gave the river its name. Only one of the thirty mills that once dotted the river remains today for canoeists to observe. However, many of the dams associated with the mill operation remain in place. There are also a number of singular, ornate bridges, which were designed and built by A. M. Kennedy, a master of bridge building.

Teamwork: the wife maneuvers the canoe while her husband fishes for dinner.

Along Flatrock's lower reaches is a twenty-three-mile section that offers a canoe trip of moderate difficulty and requires about seven hours of paddling. The put-in is at the Route 9 bridge, approximately two miles north of Norristown or about ten miles south of Shelbyville. In addition to the two dams there are several log obstructions and rock dams that have been partially washed out, making progress difficult during low water levels. There is very little development in this stretch, and the banks and hills are softened by trees that include box elder, sycamore, silver maple, cottonwood, ash, and elm. Willows hold on for dear life to the sandbar islands and gravel bars. Ahead of the canoe wood ducks, sandpipers, kingfishers, and small songbirds are flushed to flight. In 1974 the sighting of an osprey generated considerable interest among the locals, as this species is rapidly diminishing in the area.

Near Columbus at the Route 31 bridge is the recommended takeout. The southeast corner of the bridge is the best path up to your car, which can be parked on the road shoulder on the east side of the river. There are no public picnic or campground facilities along this canoe trail, but complete facilities are available at Millrace Park in Columbus, south of the takeout point.

Blue River

This river originates in Washington County in southern Indiana and flows through one of the most scenic, interesting, and diverse areas of the state. From your canoe you will see rural farmsteads, pastoral tranquility, extensive forests, numerous caves, and limestone in many forms. Blue River is an entrenched stream whose current has cut deep into the limestone bedrock over the centuries. A series of "half canyons" lie astride the stream, never completely enclosing it. The region is typical of a karst (limestone) topography and is characterized by many sinkholes and caves formed as the water dissolved the rock. The imposing limestone walls along the paddling route are usually softened by a heavy cover of trees, shrubs, and vines.

The beauty of the Blue River basin was explored by Squire Boone, Daniel's brother. He found large Indian populations whose dwelling sites can still be traced.

An interesting but rugged trip is the stretch from Fredericksburg to Milltown, with put-in at the site of the abandoned bridge in town. This trip is a rather strenuous twenty-four-mile cruise, but the scenery makes it worthwhile. Rock is a constant feature of the streambed, but much of it is covered by sediment. However, the rock and gravel bars are exposed in the fast water of the rapids. The canoeist must remain alert for submerged boulders, which can dent or scrape a canoe. The river is up to eighty-five feet wide and has an average depth of about five feet. The rapids come from a fall of about four feet per mile.

The takeout point is at the old iron bridge in Milltown, on the right bank. Immediately adjacent to the bridge is a dam that requires a portage on the right side.

Indiana canoe trails ramble through typical midwestern country: 'coon and 'possum bottomlands; sycamore, hickory, and Osage orange stands; rocky hills; and rich river bottom soil that supports tall trees where the rare pileated woodpecker thrives. You can get completely lost and turn your back on civilization paddling Hoosier streams. The natural beauty of streams differs from locale to locale, but the potential for peace and serenity can be found in all.

Information Sources

Indiana Canoe Guide, is available from the Department of Natural Resources, 616 State Office Bldg., Indianapolis, Indiana 46204. This guide offers a description of twenty-one rivers, access points, dams, campsites, and so on.

Index to Topographic Maps of Indiana is available from the Department of Natural Resources, Map Sales Unit, Room 604, State Office Building, Indianapolis, Indiana 46204.

Camping in Indiana is available from the Department of Natural Resources, 616 State Office Building., Indianapolis, Indiana 46204.

Indiana Trout Streams and Lakes is available from the Division of Fish and Game, 607 State Office Building., Indianapolis, Indiana 46204.

Indiana Historical Map (for history buffs) is available from the Division of Parks, 616 State Office Building, Indianapolis, Indiana 46204.

4

Adventure Trails of Iowa

Called "beautiful land" by the Indians, Iowa, in its entirety, is an undulating prairie that rises gradually from east to west. It is bordered by two of the country's largest rivers—the Mississippi on the east and the Missouri on the west.

History indicates that the first white men to set foot on Iowa soil were Pere Marquette and Louis Jolliet in 1673 when they canoed to the junction of the Wisconsin and Mississippi rivers near the present town of McGregor. The Illini Indians were dominant during this period but were decimated by the Sacs and Foxes, who were led by their chieftans, Black Hawk and Keokuk.

In the late 1700s the white settler Julien DuBuque established a lead mining camp at the site of the city that bears his name. Iowa was formally declared French territory by LaSalle (1682) and in 1803 was acquired by the United States as part of the Louisiana Purchase.

Iowa Canoe Trails

The charm of Iowa rivers lies in their variety. It is this variety that adds spice and splash to the Iowa canoeing trip. The state's canoe trails range from meandering streams through farmland and meadow to others that race between tunneled banks of cliffs or are arcaded by arching trees. And then there are the broad-channeled, ship-carrying waterways—the Missouri and the Mississippi—that serve as a vital link in joining the Atlantic Ocean to the Gulf of Mexico.

Some of Iowa's rivers carry dim legends of buried treasure; others are waterways with lurid pasts; others have national and local historic sites; and still others are pure water trout streams. The canoeist determines the duration of an Iowa trip by the amount of time the paddle will be at rest while fishing, exploring, digging for treasure, taking pictures, or chatting with local residents.

Upper Iowa River

Meandering through one of the deepest valleys in the state, the Upper Iowa offers a leisurely float; frequent stops permit the canoeist to leave the craft and wade for fish. The streambed of limestone rubble and sand provides firm footing, and its clean, cool water from numerous springs adds up to a fisher's delight. The stretch south of Kendallville is one of the scenic highlights of the state. When did you last see a suspension bridge? There is one here, erected by the county for local children to cross on their way to and from school.

The trip on the upper stretch of the river from Lime Springs to Kendallville has its devotees. Canoeists cruise mostly during spring and early summer, when the water is high. Fishers favor the river at all times, because the sandbars, deep holes, and runs where the fish congregate are easily spotted and accessible.

Take Route 63 to Lime Springs and then go one mile north of the town to the put-in point, which is on a rocky point below the bridge, on the right bank. The trip ahead is about twenty-four river miles and requires fourteen or more hours of paddling and floating time, adding up to a leisurely weekend trip. The launching area is at the site of the original Lime Springs, now called "old town"; it is marked by a cluster of buildings and a dam that was built in 1855. About four miles downstream is the Foreston Bridge, where there is another site of an early mill; the crumbling remains of the mill dam can still be seen near the bridge. About three miles below the Foreston Bridge the river deepens and quickens as it bears sharply to the east. This is a very scenic stretch of the river with heavily wooded, wild banks. Turning the eyes back to the river is necessary, as there is a stretch of large rocks and sandbars and a series of rapids and pools.

In the next four miles the river crosses the Minnesota state line in several places; this gives youngsters in the party the opportunity of bragging to pals that they canoed two states on their trip. Just below the next county road bridge are the remains of the old concrete Florenceville dam. The river divides here, and the left (west) channel will take you around without a portage. About three miles away on the right side there is an ideal campsite facing a beautiful rocky bluff. The fishing in this water is touted as great, which may be an incentive to stop over for the night. A large spring, Odessa, is just below, flowing out of a cave about thirty feet from the left bank of the river proper.

About five miles farther downstream is the Larkin Bridge, where the character of the river changes from flatland to the more rugged limestone rock country that is typical of the river below Kendallville. In the next seven miles or so there are three bridges that are passed before the takeout point in a timber pasture on the right bank above the Kendallville bridge.

The trip from Kendallville to Decorah is a charm; the scenery is great and there is trout water, a waterfall, and fast and slow water current. The total distance is about

Limestone rock country, with its clean, scenic, and challenging rivers, is typical of many Iowa canoe trails.
(Old Town Canoe Company, Old Town, Maine)

thirty river miles, which makes an easy two-day trip. Blufftown is about the halfway point, and since there is a campsite there, it makes a convenient objective for the first day. For those who do not wish to camp out, excellent overnight accommodations are available at Cresco and Decorah. The canoe-camper will find many likely campsites along the river.

The put-in point is on the north side of the river, above the Kendallville bridge, and one-fourth mile away is the suspension footbridge mentioned earlier. In the next seven miles there are three bridges and a long, prominent sandbar on the right bank at the foot of a vertical limestone wall. The river then horseshoes back so sharply that it resembles a giant arrowhead. At the north point of the arrowhead a sparkling little trout stream, Coldwater Creek, enters the river from the left bank through a parklike meadow. Below the feeder creek, along the left bank, are the spectacular Chimney Rocks—massive pillars of stone 50 feet in diameter and 200 feet high. Soon after, there appears the impressive limestone walls near Bluffton bridge. There is a possible takeout point on the left bank below the bridge. The Bluffton store, where refreshments are available, is about one-fourth mile east of the bridge, on the left side of the river.

From Bluffton to the south and east the land along the massive rock wall is owned by the state. It was purchased to preserve the balsam fir trees. Below Twin Bridge is the largest rapid of the trip, and in low water conditions it may be necessary to make a short carryover. After the fast water there is a distinct change in the river; the bluffs gradually recede, the river widens, the current slackens, and shallow stretches become more frequent.

More than five miles downstream of Twin Bridge, on the left bank, is a beautiful waterfall known as Malanaphy Springs. The area offers an interesting stopover to explore and makes a nice spot for lunch. Six and one-half miles downstream, located back from the river, to the left on the high ground, loom the buildings of Luther College. Past several attractive homes with views of the river, the bridge offers a recommended takeout point on the left side.

Iowa River

This is a typical prairie stream—shallow and gently curving —but in some stretches it races between confining cliffs of limestone. The town of Steamboat Rock brought two to three thousand prospectors to its shore in 1850, when a trace of gold was panned from the sand. Iowa's only "Gold Rush" did not, however, develop into a bonanza.

A claim that keeps recurring is that the dense timberland downriver served as a hideout for Jesse James and his gang. The high elevations at Steamboat and Tower Rocks project from the shores to offer long, impressive views.

North of Alden is Bigelow Park, which provides an excellent place to put in, as there are picnic and sanitation facilities. A few miles south, at Bessman–Kemp Park, canoeists find picnic and sanitation facilities as well as camping. The river's flow is sluggish at the outset due to the backed-up water from the Alden dam. The portage is made at the north end of the dam. The Mormon Bridge commemorates the Emmett party of pioneers, which suffered from cold, exposure, and lack of provisions on their westward trek during the severe winter of 1844–45. Many of their number were buried in unmarked graves.

Limestone-sculptured banks are found on the Iowa River and many others of the state's streams.

A brief stretch of the river from the dam to Iowa Falls gives a preview of the limestone sculptured banks to follow. First, however, the moving water is stilled again by the dam one-mile west of Iowa Falls. The portage is on the right bank, where a steep path ends just below the overflow chute. Some canoeists prefer to begin their trip here.

On the meandering stream again the bluffs sculptured by wind and water display many different formations. The remnants of an old mill on the left bank date back to pioneer days. Several narrow, fast channels have fences stretched across the river, calling for alertness by the paddlers. Below Cross Ford Bridge the county conservation board has a twenty-six-acre area that provides landing and camping.

The river makes a huge oxbow curve to the left toward Eagle City, a historic place. Here are found the remains of one of the oldest mills of pioneer days. Just below the bridge is a seventy-acre county park that provides picnicking, camping, access, and adequate parking. From Eagle City past Huse Bridge to Hardin City, the way courses through the heart of the "Iowa River Green Belt." Several county recreational areas lie in the area and provide access and camping for canoeists. The river varies in depth and flow rate, and fences may also be encountered in this stretch.

From Hardin City to Steamboat Rock the cruise continues through the "Green Belt" with hills covered with thick stands of native trees sloping down to the water. Here, too, are several of the county-controlled areas that invite exploration. Near Steamboat Rock are the sites of early gold rushes and coal mining. Small amounts of gold are still found, and local prospectors still pan a small amount of gold each year. As you approach Steamboat Rock, the grounds of the Iowa River Recreation Association on the right provide landing, picnicking, and camping areas. The portage at Steamboat Rock, at the left end of the dam, is easily managed.

Another county park at the south edge of Steamboat Rock contains remnants of the rock formations for which the town was named as well as Tower Rock, which rises over sixty feet and is covered with dates and initials of covered wagon passengers dating back 100 years. Paddling in the shadows of abrupt limestone bluffs, you pass under Coal Bank Hill Bridge and on to Pine Lake State Park at Eldora, the end of the trip. Take out here unless fishing is on the program. The river slows and shallows at this point—all the better to work a fishing lure in the weed pockets.

Little Sioux River

This river served the Plains Indians as a route to the pipestone quarries of Minnesota. Pipestone was used to handcraft the Indian calumet, or peace pipe. The Little Sioux also knew the paddle of the voyageurs who freighted the furs from northern regions. Pilot Rock, south of Cherokee, served as a trail marker for the covered wagon trains. According to archeologists, the Mill Creek Indian culture dates back to A.D. 1200. As a canoeist on the Little Sioux you have an opportunity to contribute to Iowa history research; in co-operation with the Sanford Museum in Cherokee, many individuals have become Little Sioux history buffs and have made contributions to the museum's research.

One excellent trip is from Linn Grove to Cherokee. The total distance is about thirty-five miles, an easy two-day trip, but a third day should be added for fishing and exploring. The water levels are capricious, but neither dams nor rapids of any consequence slow the cruise. However, good campsites are scarce because of the high banks. The put-in is just below the main dam at Linn Grove on the left, or south, shore. There are several places downriver where the water divides into two or more channels. In general, take the channel carrying the most water. One exception to this occurs about six miles below Linn Grove, where the right channel should be taken.

Three miles north of where Waterman Creek enters the Little Sioux is the site of one of the Mill Creek Indian villages. A mile farther is the general vicinity where Ink-paduta and his band of renegade Sioux Indians camped in 1857 en route to the bloodiest Indian outbreak in Iowa's history, the Spirit Lake Massacre. As the miles pass by, you will see a dredged and straightened channel, a possible sandbar campsite, continuing high bluffs, three county conservation board access areas, and the point below Stoner's Bridge where Mill Creek enters the river. Several ancient village sites have been discovered on the banks here. One mile below the White Mill Bridge is the Route 3 bridge at Cherokee, and one-half mile farther on is a convenient takeout point on the left bank above the Route 59 bridge. Anyone interested in the history of the region should visit the Sanford Museum in Cherokee. This laudable community cultural center is devoted to the geological and archeological history of the Little Sioux Valley.

Wapsi River

The Wapsi's name stems from "Wapsipinicon," or "Swan Apple," a white artichoke that grew along its shores during Indian times. Along the course of this, the longest river in northeast Iowa, lies the village of Waubeek. This village was settled in the 1850s by New England whaling families who migrated far inland to avoid any temptation for husbands and sons to work the strenuous, dangerous whaling fleets. They named their newly adopted township "Maine" in honor of their old home and brought their culture with them, placing emblems reminiscent of their maritime way of life over the doorways. Visitors may still see the ivory-tipped harpoons, storm lamps, and ships' bells over the doorways of the New England style homes, placed in memory of an adventurous, but forsaken, way of life.

The Wapsi's headwaters are just above the Minnesota state line. From there the river drifts into Iowa and then southeasterly to the Mississippi River. A popular canoe trip is the fifty-mile, two- to three-day run from Independence (Routes 150 and 20) to Stone City. The put-in point at Independence is on the right bank, upstream of the Route 150 bridge. On a slow, meandering current it is six miles to the Old Iron Bridge. The flat country continues for about five miles to the six-foot recreational dam at the town of

Quasqueton, so named from the Indian word *Quasqetuck*, which means "swift running water."

In an earlier day the present-day town site served as the junction of many Indian trails. The present Stone City dates back to 1842. The portage around the dam is on the right side. Approximately ten miles downstream is Troy Mills bridge and dam, which is portaged on the right. From there it is slightly over thirteen miles to the Central City bridge, where Route 13 crosses the river. The dam below is portaged on the left. The river is often quite shallow at the put-in point and most likely will require getting out of the canoe and pulling it along. In the next six-mile stretch the riverbank scenery improves, the valley narrows, and the country becomes wild with steep, heavily wooded bluffs.

The river later skirts the north side of Waubeek. In addition to its maritime origins, the town has another claim to fame: It is the birthplace of poet and author Jay Sigmund. A county park is named in his honor.

Below Waubeek the river divides into a series of small, shallow channels, most of which are blocked by fallen trees and beaver dams. It is probably best to pull the canoe over the obstacles or to portage. If you must take out, the best carryover is through the timbered pasture on the left bank. The trip ends at Stone City, ten miles downstream. The takeout is on the right side, just above the bridge. Do not hurry from this picturesque little village. Stone City, renowned for its stone quarries, produced the finest limestone in the state, and its stone adorns the old state capitol in Iowa City.

Boone River

Some interesting history is associated with the Boone, which passes Indian burial grounds; the riverside mills of Old Bone, Tunnel, and Bell; deep caves; and other ancient structures. Old Bone's Mill, built in 1854, has a colorful past, including continual battles with ice in the winter and floods in the spring; being a center for grinding grain for local farmers; a dash of romantic hanky-panky, with the miller's wife being whisked away; and even an unsolved murder. Below Bell's Mill there is another Boone River legend, which involves a cave with fallen-away steps. Explorer's have sought but never found a fabulous treasure reputed to be buried here. When conditions are right, the Boone offers a pleasant, absorbing canoeing experience. To immediately get into the most interesting stretch of the river, put in just above the Bever Bridge on the left bank. Soon you will be floating near the site of Old Bone's Mill, which brings to mind its intrigue and romance. The eyebrow-raising tenure of Bone's Mill ended in a thunderous explosion that ended its existence, but not its legend.

The natural aspects of the river are interesting, too. There is good catfish and smallmouth bass fishing. Hilly banks form huge rock walls that rise more than 20 feet and extend 200 feet downriver. Also, there are Indian burial sites, swallow nests sculptured in mud cling to the cliffs; and always the tireless current carries you along.

Bell's Mill Park is the site of a mill built by a Methodist preacher, David Eckerson, in 1853. On March 2, 1888, the new owner of the mill, Benjamin Bell, died, and that night floodwaters swept away the dam and destroyed the mill. Mr. and Mrs. Jasper Bell, heirs to the property, donated the land for the present county park as a memorial to the pioneers who settled the area.

Downstream at Haskell Bridge you will get a long view of the verdant valley and the road beyond, which winds up and over the distant hill. About five minutes later you will come to Vegor Bridge, and high on a scenic hill to the north is the Vegor Cemetery, a final resting place first of Indians and later of the settlers. After several more minutes of paddling, the Boone loses its identity as it flows into the Des Moines River. A mile or so below the junction and below Belleville Bridge is an excellent takeout point. Stratford, on Route 175, is nearby.

From a high vantage point, it is possible to enjoy a peaceful river scene.

Des Moines River

Of the 500-mile course of the Des Moines River, the short trip from Kalo to Lehigh (eleven miles) is a scenic attraction and cruising treat. It has a moderate current, neither dams nor portages, and lots of history. There is Boneyard Hollow, for example, where the Indians drove buffalo, deer, and elk from the adjacent prairies to and over the cliffs to their death in order to collect the meat, hides, and bones.

This trip is an ideal one-day excursion. It involves about three and one-half hours of comfortable paddling, leaving plenty of time for fishing, lazing, and exploring the many inviting and intriguing places along the way. In times of extremely low water the cruise will take a little longer, because it will be necessary to get your feet wet by wading a few sandbars and leading the canoe around other obstructions.

The recommended put-in is at Kalo, located six and one-half miles below Fort Dodge. It can be reached by driving four miles south from Route 20 on Route 169 and then three miles through Otho and swinging northeast to Kalo. Enter the river on the left bank, facing downstream, just below the highway bridge.

The river bears east for a few miles, where you will see several small streams and their deeply cut sandstone wall banks—all of which provide interesting gorges to explore. In one such opening is Wildcat Cave, which consists of several shallow chambers gouged out of the soft sandstone. A low rock wall of scenic interest overhangs the left bank. Farther along you skirt high bluffs of sandstone. Through one such bluff a small stream has cut an imposing gorge that is now the site of Woodman's Hollow State Preserve. Downstream, in a setting of bluffs and ravines that extend from the river, is the beginning of the Dolliver Memorial State Park, which extends for a considerable distance on the right bank. A convenient stopover for canoeists is near the shelter house and public campgrounds. This is a spot of great natural beauty with many places of interest. The setting is rural and wild, with the lively Prairie Creek twisting its way through the soft rock of the region. The landscape is embroidered by a unique variety of trees and plants, especially ferns, which give softness to the ravines. Here is the site of Boneyard Hollow, a few hundred yards upstream from the landing. This deep ravine is fairly wide at its entrance near the river, but as it extends back, it narrows into a canyonlike gorge and fans out into several smaller ravines. Abrupt sandstone ledges rise fifty to seventy-five feet on either side, the bottoms of which were found to contain great quantities of animal bones, Indian arrowheads, axes and other weapons, and implements that were unearthed in the hollow by early settlers.

The beds of copperas (hydrated ferrous sulfate) are another must to see in the park. They are found in a sandstone bluff 150 feet high and several hundred feet long, located but a short distance from the river. Along with this unusual deposit of minerals, there are many exposed petrified plants. Legend indicates that the Indians used the multicolored copperas powder for war paint, and the early pioneers used it to color the cloth for their clothing.

On resuming the trip on a southeasterly course, after three to four miles the Lehigh Bridge is reached. Here the water has been backed up by a low head rock dam built across the river just above the bridge. The dam has an interesting background; it was constructed over a seven-year period as a community project by a group of Lehigh residents to assist in maintaining the water level upstream for improved boating and fishing. The takeout point is on the left, or downstream, side, just above the Lehigh Bridge, where there is a convenient parking lot. There is access to Route 50 and then to Route 169.

Raccoon River

In Iowa getting away from it all is best achieved by canoeing the Raccoon. The route, which flows through heavily

Fishing a quiet bay of the backed-up water of a dam is often rewarding.

timbered land, is not marred by population clusters and fosters a far-from-civilization feeling. The remains of a grist mill with millstones brought by oxen from Pennsylvania in 1858 can be seen along the river.

The central Iowa Raccoon River trip that is most floated is the stretch from Jefferson to Adel—a fine weekend trip. The distance is approximately forty-six miles, in which the river flows through heavily timbered bottomland. Most of the bridges are far apart, which adds to that hinterland feeling. Over the entire route there is a good volume of water; exposed gravel and sandbars make passable campsites. There are neither dangerous rapids nor dams nor other normal obstructions to be pulled over or portaged. At all times, however, caution should be exercised when wading, as there are unexpected deep dropoffs.

The place to put in is south of Jefferson, at the Henderson County Park, near the Route 4 bridge. At the outset the river runs strong and clean; however, there are a few fences to contend with. Constant vigilance with the eyes riveted ahead will keep you out of trouble.

It is about seven and one-half miles to Squirrel Hollow Park, the area where the Hardin and Buttrick creeks drain into the Raccoon River from the left bank. Squirrel Hollow is a place for reconnoitering. Maintained by the Greene County Conservation Board, it was developed in the 1930s under the Civilian Conservation Corps program. The park is located on the summit of a steep bluff commanding a splendid view of a westerly sweeping bend in the river. The park's stone shelter can be reached from the river by a stone stairway cut into the face of the bluff. The previously mentioned millstones, brought from Pennsylvania by Josh Locke for the early Coon Valley Mill, have been set for posterity in the floor of the shelter.

The river continues on a winding, narrowing course with occasional, seasonal driftwood jams in the bends of the river. Approximately seven miles along, the Raccoon makes a looping northeasterly turn past the towering clay and rock bluffs for about six miles to the Davey Hill Bridge west of the town of Perry.

Note: Perry represents the psychological, if not geographic, midpoint of the trip. For a one-day float, this would be the takeout point. When starting from Jefferson, this would be the put-in point for the trip to Adel.

The deep, fast water in this stretch offers the best fishing, according to local residents.

Past several closely spaced bridges, the flow of the river slows on the approach to the upper dam above Abel. It is about two miles to the takeout point at Riverside Park via the west channel.

Turkey River

It is likely that the only portage in all of recreational canoeing that requires the canoeist to tote his craft down the main street of a town is in Elkader. The Turkey River dam above town and another below, require this unique cross-town carry. There are, however, some attendant advantages; the town offers an excellent hotel, restaurants, ice cream, cold drinks, and, perhaps, the forgotten suntan lotion. Should you plan a Saturday trip, it would be wise to arrange for a car or truck to transport canoe and gear in order not to completely disrupt the town's business.

Without portaging Main Street in Elkader, homemakers living on the river can go shopping via the water route.
(Switzer Studio, Concordia, Kansas)

In the "Little Switzerland" area of northeastern Iowa, the Turkey River is its largest, with a 135-mile sweep through four counties before entering the Mississippi below the Guttenberg dam. The most popular canoeing segment lies within the middle section of the river, roughly from Spillville to Elkport, where the current is strong, the river bottom rocky, and the banks made of limestone.

The stretch of the Turkey that canoeists seem to prefer runs from Elgin through Elkader to Garber. Along the route the narrow valley is bounded by hardwood trees interspersed with red cedar and by the rugged bluffs that seem to be the trademark of northern Iowa streams. The rate of fall ranges from about four to six feet per mile, which makes for a consistent, interesting flow. There are no difficult or dangerous rapids. However, there are occasional floating logs, branches, and trees that get hung up in the bends of the river.

If you face downstream, the put-in at Elgin is at the bridge abutment on the left bank of the upstream side. Once launched, you immediately cross the river above the bridge to the right bank, where the main channel flows. From here the distance to Garber is approximately thirty-four river miles, just right for a weekend trip. Floating along mile after mile on a strong current, you observe the half-mile-wide, rich river valley. About eight miles down is the only highway bridge to be seen in this first stretch. Below the bridge the valley narrows and the river races. Four miles later the Big Springs water flows into the river on the left, where there is a state trout hatchery. About two hours later you are in the quieted water backed up by the Elkader Dam. The takeout is at the athletic field on the right bank, 150 yards above the power dam. Then comes the portage down the main street of town.

One is immediately impressed by the aura of Elkader, a typically clean, friendly Iowa town. In addition to the Turkey River, which goes directly through town, its image is enhanced by history. The remains of a mill built in 1849 near the old and famous Keystone Arch bridge and the imposing, white-towered Clayton County Courthouse dominate the center of town.

To get back on the water trail, the put-in requires a long carry of about three city blocks to the Riverside Park because of a second smaller dam. The valley below Elkader continues to reveal natural beauty as well as man-made progress in the prosperous and diversified farms. Downstream, Roberts Creek enters the river from the left. Farther down on the left bank are the remains of the old mill town of Motor. The picturesque mill, with its massive stone walls, worn millstones, and hand-hewn beams, is in an excellent state of preservation. It was built of native limestone by John Thompson in 1864.

Below Motor the current is fast, with rapids directly under the bridge. The river then makes several sharp turns between the steep, heavily wooded bluffs that seem to close in on the river. About five miles below Motor Bridge is a particularly sharp bend known as Devil's Elbow. It is marked by two large pine trees on the right-hand bluff at the turn, giving a clue that the turbulence is near. The shallow rapids below are easily run. In low water some wading and pulling of the canoe may be necessary. Approximately five miles down the river open farmland replaces the hill country. Shortly thereafter the Volga River can be seen entering from the right. Only one-half mile more and you are at the bridge at Garber. The takeout point is on the right bank, below the bridge.

Note. In discussing the Rock River in the Illinois chapter, it was indicated that a "package" type of canoe trip was available, utilizing riverside hotels, restaurants, stores, and so on. This type of trip frees the traveler from the responsibilities of planning, packing, obtaining provisions, and sleeping out. Today there is an increasing interest in this type of trip for fishing, skiing, sightseeing, and many other activities.

Elkader offers an efficiently structured package trip for canoeists.* The Alpine Inn offers a "package plan" for the trip discussed above that includes canoe rental, spotting, and pickup. The complete coverage also includes two breakfasts, dinners off the regular menu, lodging for two nights, and box lunches for a picnic-style noon meal on the river. The price for the trip, including housing and meals, is lower than if the items were paid for separately.

---

*Information can be obtained from the Alpine Inn, Elkader, Iowa 52043, phone (319) 245-1010. The manager, Lloyd Gossman, is also a resource person for general information on the canoeing picture in this "Little Switzerland" complex of interesting streams.

Other Iowa Rivers

Most canoeists are collectors of rivers. Therefore, here is a capsule description of a few more Iowa rivers.

Volga River

This is an out-of-the-way river that has seen only a few canoes in the last decade. A tough river, the Volga rushes through a deep, narrow, and twisting valley, confined by high, heavily wooded, rolling hills and precipitous rock cliffs. The water rises rapidly after a rain, fluctuating as much as six feet in this narrow valley. Thus it becomes treacherous due to the added factors of sharp turns and floating debris. In the lower stretches the Volga slows in the shallow areas, and canoeists may have to step out and carry the craft over the rocks. Osborne Plantation, a county area located on Route 13 to Garber, is seventeen miles away, an overnight trip. The fishing is good, the scenery is spectacular, and there is much wildlife. But the Volga is not for the weak of muscle or heart.

Yellow River

This river was called "LeJaun Riviere" by the French voyagers who paddled it as early as the 1700s. After a rain the water becomes discolored from the washed-down soil pigments; hence the name "yellow." On the banks of this "Little Switzerland" river and in its forty-mile valley a lot of history has unfolded: the first water mill in the state and an Indian mission school were both established in the 1830s; Effigy Mounds National Monument is nearby; and the area saw the decade of mills—grist, flour, lumber, wood—in the 1850s. The river's rate of fall is mind- and muscle-boggling, as it varies from six feet per mile to about twenty-five, in the vicinity of Ion Bridge. The water is not deep, but the rapids are frequent, fast, and rocky, and you will leave a lot of paint or aluminum on the immovable rocks. Volney to the Mississippi River, eighteen miles, is a one-day adventure.

Red Cedar River

With its wild scenery and excellent fishing, the Red Cedar River has a rate of fall of only about three feet per mile, which eliminates the possibility of rough rapids. The forty-one-mile stretch from Otranto to Charles City is the most heavily traveled. Portages are required at three power dams, one beautiful with a low footbridge. Excellent feeder streams that harbor bass and trout are numerous, there are many red cedar and hardwood stands on the limestone cliffs, and the bottomlands are heavily forested.

At Mitchell the dam is on the site of a mill dating from 1865, the millstones of which have been built into the powerhouse wall. The keystone of the powerhouse is from the Paragon Woolen Mill, built around 1865. At Spring Park's lower end there is a low rock "Beauty Dam" backing up the water from an enclosed spring. For canoeing, fishing, camping, and wild scenery, the Red Cedar ranks with the best.

Information Sources

"Iowa Canoe Trips" is available from the Iowa Conservation Commission, 300 Fourth St., Des Moines, Iowa 50319.

"Your Guide to Iowa Trout Waters" is available from the Iowa Conservation Commission, 300 Fourth St., Des Moines, Iowa 50319.

"Iowa Camping and Recreation Areas" is available from the Iowa Conservation Commission, 300 Fourth St., Des Moines, Iowa 50319.

"A Guide to the Upper Iowa River," by George E. Knudson, Luther College, Decorah, Iowa, gives a more detailed account of a canoe trip on the Upper Iowa River.

5

Adventure Trails of Michigan

The state of Michigan is cut in two by Lake Michigan and Lake Huron; the sparsely populated upper peninsula is a rolling, rocky land, largely forested. The lower peninsula varies from fertile farmland and orchards in the south to the extensive cutover forests and many small lakes and clean rivers farther north.

At the time of the French explorers' arrival, the region was populated by tribes of the Algonquin and Iroquois. The Ottowas, largest of the Algonquin group in Michigan, were once led by the great Chief Pontiac.

In 1612, Etienne Brule reported reaching the region now known as Georgian Bay in Ontario, Canada. In 1621, he explored part of Lake Superior, where he found the Huron Indians mining copper. In 1634, Jean Nicolet visited the present site of Sault Ste. Marie and explored the country west of Green Bay. He was followed by Father Pere Marquette (1668), who founded the first permanent mission and settlement at Sault Ste. Marie. In 1671, Marquette established a mission among the Huron at St. Ignace. Later, various French explorers visited the southern reaches of the state. In 1679, LaSalle established Fort Miamis at the mouth of the St. Joseph River. In 1690, Father Aveneau explored the upper reaches of the St. Joseph and established a mission near Niles. Cadillac first settled Detroit in 1701. On and on through the 1600s we see the historic probes into Michigan, mostly by the canoes of French explorers, missionaries, fur traders, and Indian guides.

Michigan Canoe Trails

The water trails of the Wolverine state knew the birchbark canoe long before they floated the bateaus of the French explorers. Indians, voyageurs, settlers, loggers, and, now, recreationists have enjoyed the state's moving waters, which have retained much of their integrity to this day. Clean and challenging, Michigan's streams are dispersed over all sections of the state, including the upper peninsula. Canoe liveries are at strategic locations throughout the state, assuring a pleasant excursion. Though fast moving, most streams are shallow and safe for the average canoeist, as water depth seldom exceeds a person's height.

The most dependable recommendation of a river is that it is used extensively by the local canoeists. Michigan rivers are a case in point; some canoe trails have become so popular that canoe traffic on a summer weekend can be called congested. The Pere Marquette, Manistee, Au Sauble, and Pine rivers are examples.

Michigan's Department of Natural Resources has thoroughly checked out the various rivers and lakes designated as canoe trails and has identified approximately forty-four canoe trips by location, length, and difficulty. Sources of supplies and availability of canoes for rent are also listed. The canoe trails of Michigan will be discussed in the following order: first

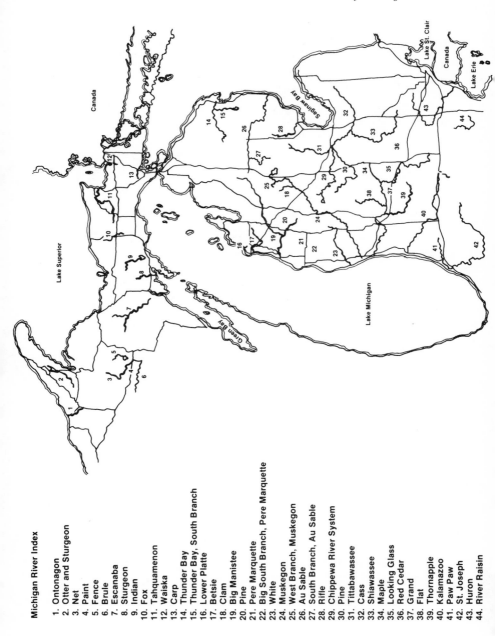

Michigan River Index

1. Ontonagon
2. Otter and Sturgeon
3. Net
4. Paint
5. Fence
6. Brule
7. Escanaba
8. Sturgeon
9. Indian
10. Fox
11. Tahquamenon
12. Waiska
13. Carp
14. Thunder Bay
15. Thunder Bay, South Branch
16. Lower Platte
17. Betsie
18. Clam
19. Big Manistee
20. Pine
21. Pere Marquette
22. Big South Branch, Pere Marquette
23. White
24. Muskegon
25. West Branch, Muskegon
26. Au Sable
27. South Branch, Au Sable
28. Rifle
29. Chippewa River System
30. Pine
31. Tittabawassee
32. Cass
33. Shiawassee
34. Maple
35. Looking Glass
36. Red Cedar
37. Grand
38. Flat
39. Thornapple
40. Kalamazoo
41. Paw Paw
42. St. Joseph
43. Huron
44. River Raisin

those of the upper peninsula, then the northern lower peninsula, and finally those of the southern lower peninsula.

Many of Michigan's Upper Peninsula rivers flow through sparsely populated, wild country.
(Michigan Tourist Council)

Net River

The fifteen-mile stretch of the Net in the upper peninsula is best experienced in two days. En route you will cruise through uninhabited wild country and through second-growth hardwoods and small swamps—all representative of inspiring upper peninsula scenery.

To get to the start of the trip, go twelve miles north of Amasa on Route 141, then one mile west on Park Siding Road to the bridge take-in. About three and one-half miles down is the Widewaters section—a stretch recommended for northern pike fishing. Maintaining a slow drift and utilizing the current and/or wind while casting ahead into undisturbed water is a good method to fish while underway.

A portage around a dam comes next, and about five miles

downstream is Chipmunk Falls, which also calls for a portage. After three more miles and another portage at Snake Rapids, you have another three-mile paddle to the Paint River, which will be discussed next. There are rentals and resource people at Crystal Falls and at Amasa.

Paint River

Some renowned anglers have rated this river as "outstanding" for smallmouth bass. Gibbs City is the suggested starting point for this forty-five mile cruise, or portion thereof. You will cruise for about thirteen miles before the portage at Hemlock Rapids. Should you desire a shorter run of the Paint, there is an adequate put-in or takeout spot at a county highway bridge three miles below Hemlock Rapids. Five miles downstream is Chicagon Slough, where fishing for northerns is best on the right-hand shore. Another five miles and the Paint crosses Route 141, and about three miles farther is the Crystal Falls power dam, where you take out. Should you wish to continue, it will be necessary to arrange to have a truck haul canoes and gear to the Route 69 bridge, after which you will be in slow backwater that is impounded by the Little Bull Rapids power dam. After another portage around Horserace Rapids, the Paint joins the Brule River. About two miles down there is a cleared campsite that has access to Routes 2 and 141 and is a good stopover regardless of how much of the river you use.

Brule River

This forty-seven mile river is a canoeist's dream; it is not overpowering and has only a few mild rapids. It is also prime trout water, and through the years some very large trout have been taken from the Brule. Put-in is at Route 73 about ten miles southwest of Iron River; eleven miles downstream from that point is the Route 189 bridge. Several miles more and the red-colored water from the Iron River discolors the

Brule, but the trout fishing is unaffected. There are several takeout points up to where the Brule joins the Paint River to form the Menominee River. Because the Brule is a Wisconsin–Michigan boundary water, special fishing regulations are in effect; they are covered in *Michigan Rules for Fishing*, which will be issued to you when you purchase a license. Canoes, pickups, and information are available at Crystal Falls or Iron River.

The Fox, Indian, and Carp Rivers

If you are a trout fishing canoeist, there are three rivers to try your fly rod and paddle on: the Fox, Indian, and Carp rivers.

THE FOX. The seventeen-mile Fox River offers brook trout action. The put-in is at the historic town of Seney, one of Michigan's rip-roaring lumber towns of an earlier era. If you wish to fish the river in leisurely style, campsites and accesses are numerous on the way to Germfask (on Route 77), where you should end your trip.

THE INDIAN. The Indian River supports brook, brown, and rainbow trout. For fifty miles this river has no difficult water, and takeout spots are numerous. After the put-in at the U.S. Forest Service Widewater Campground, a good campsite for the first night is at Indian River Campground. The end of the action with trout is the boat landing at Indian Lake on the immediate right side; Route 149 leads to the landing.

THE CARP. A little farther east, the twenty-mile Carp River also offers brook, brown, and rainbow trout fishing. Put in at the Route 123 bridge, which is about six miles north of Moran, and cruise through sparsely settled land. A short rapids below Platz Lake Outlet should offer little or no problems. Takeout is at St. Martin Bay, and Route 75 is nearby for loading canoe and gear.

Tahquamenon River

The sixty-three-mile Tahquamenon offers a week's cruise through an idyllic wilderness. It is characterized by an interplay of marsh and forest flora, rock formations, virgin trees, wildlife, and waterfowl. Weaving through a secluded, roadless area, the river is highlighted by two waterfalls: the upper falls of the Tahquamenon are 200 feet wide, and cola-colored water cascades majestically forty-five feet. Here, as along many Michigan water trails, the canoeist tarries to savor the scenes that weave their magic on the senses. *Caution:* Don't plan your trip for June or July, for the black flies are at their fiercest then.

Begin your trip at McMillan with an early start so that you can get past the extensive willow marsh, which lacks a campsite and which lasts for some fifteen miles. The early start will also give you time to fish for northern pike in the tall, reedy, and shallow marsh. That way you will probably have fish for your evening meal. Below the marsh campsites are ample, and the only portages are at the upper and lower falls. There is fast water two miles above the lower falls, and carrying the canoe through is recommended. The best fishing for walleye, northern, rock bass, and perch is found just below the lower falls. Before starting out on this heavily timbered, high-banked, scenic river, it is recommended that detailed seasonal information be obtained from the Department of Natural Resources Office at Newberry.

Thunder Bay River

Dropping down to the northern lower peninsula, the Thunder Bay River offers many miles of clean trout fishing water, and when the current slows, one can fish for northern and bass. Put in at Lake Fifteen southwest of Alpena at Route 33. The first fifteen miles are fast and shallow trout water. The first portage is on the south side of the dam at Atlanta; then there is a short carry at the dam at Hillman. Log jams may require short carryovers below Hillman. Campsites are situated all along the river, so if you are tired, enchanted with the scenery, or desirous of spending more time fishing, you can make use of them and tarry.

From Hillman to Long Rapids are twenty-two miles of twisting river through farmland, swamps, and timbered country. This stretch also offers smallmouth bass and northern fishing. There are some tricky but not dangerous rapids for five miles below Long Rapids. The final fifteen miles of the trip are in the backwaters, and for the shortest route, keep to the north shore of Seven Mile Pond. There are short portages around the next two dams before reaching Alpena.

You can shorten or lengthen the time spent cruising Thunder Bay River. However, most trippers opt for the slow pace because it is a beautiful and interesting stream. There are many opportunities for nature and wildlife observations and photography. There are a number of housekeeping cabins on Thunder Bay, where you can clean up and rest after your trip. The Alpena Chamber of Commerce is the place to get pretrip information and advice.

Big Manistee River

The headwaters of the Manistee are at the watershed of Michigan. Slightly over 200 miles west, it empties into Lake Michigan. The Au Sauble rises but a short distance from the Manistee and flows east into Lake Huron. The first twenty-eight miles of the Manistee course through wild country with cedar swamps and log jams. The depth is one to three feet, and the water supports some trout.

The take-in at the Route 72 bridge west of Grayling, which is mile 30, is preferred by most trippers. Portage Creek joins the river from the left, and this is a good water for fishers to probe with lures. About ten miles downriver is the county bridge, and three miles beyond that is a campsite with a freshwater spring.

At mile 60 is Sharon, where the Manistee picks up more water volume from the north branch of the Manistee, along with a number of smaller creeks flowing in from both sides. A good campsite is five miles below the Route 66 bridge at Big Bend. From here it is twenty miles to the next campsite, below the Route 131 bridge, which has fresh spring water, tent sites, and so on. Another Campsite is only twelve miles of good water away, at Baxter Bridge. It is twenty twisting miles on a deepening river of four to six feet from Baxter to Harvey Bridge. The high, wooded banks and general cover support many deer, just as the deep water supports trout.

Tourists join Michiganders with complete rigs that offer housing and canoeing.

For supplies or perhaps just to stretch or use different muscles you can take out at the Route 37 bridge, secure the canoe, and walk down to Sherman. One campsite is located here, and another is five miles below, at Mesick. There is also a place to get supplies only a mile's hike away. Next you will be paddling in the backwaters of the Hodenpyl dam for eight miles, a good stretch to do some trolling for northern, bass, and panfish. The portage is on the north side of the dam (right side), and three miles below is a campsite, with several others farther down at Tippy dam. The portage is on the north side of Tippy, and the carry is about one-fourth-mile. At the dam you should get the latest information on time of water release before canoeing below this point. Released water can crest to four feet, although at that level it is still easy to ride. This occurs mostly in the early morning.

From Tippy dam it is approximately eighty miles to Manistee Lake, which marks the end of the trip. And a beautifully wild eighty miles it is, as the swift, clean water flows through the heavily forested watershed. There is an absence of human habitations, other than the farmhouses spaced far apart, as no towns straddle the banks. Traditionally this has been a stretch of water for rainbow and steelhead fishing in the fall. Now the planted coho return up the Manistee in the fall and offer a fishing adventure that was unknown a decade ago. Add the wildfowl shooting from a canoe, and truly the Manistee serves the outdoor enthusiast's needs in many ways. Takeout is at the boat dock area on the north end of Manistee Lake.

Pine River

This fifty-eight-mile, wild, tumbling river breaks down to nine miles in Wexford County, forty miles in Lake County, and nine miles in Manistee County. The Pine will keep you alert all the time. On straightaways the fast current shoots the canoe along at a joyous clip. With its four-mile-per-hour current, the river is swift, and there are many rapids and turns. It is not recommended for the novice. Novices do attempt the river, as you will discover as you come upon them swamped, upset, or grounded on sandbars. The Pine has some deep holes, but it averages out to about three feet, so canoeists temporarily stalled need not panic. They know that should something serious develop, there will soon be another canoe along in this heavily used water.

Accesses are plentiful; canoeists can put in at Edgetts,

Walker, or Skookum bridges in Lake County or at Hoxey or Peterson bridge on Route 37. Canoes and supplies are available at Baldwin, Newaygo, Wellston, and Luther. The time required to transverse the entire course is estimated at fourteen hours; you should plan to break this up into smaller segments. Most canoeists prefer the Hoxeyville bridge to the Low bridge.

Two campsites are available at Walker bridge, one on either side of the river. Popular Creek has campsites that are less improved but popular, and the Peterson bridge, about three hours below Popular Creek, has three areas reserved exclusively for canoe campers. This is a good place for an overnighter, with opportunity to swap adventure tales with fellow canoeists.

The continuation of the route to Stronach Dam does not offer the same eye-appealing diversified topography as do the upper reaches of the Pine. Because of siltation in the backwater of the dam, keep to the left for the takeout and portage. In about fifteen minutes you will arrive at the Low bridge for takeout.

In the upper peninsula rivers are in such close proximity that the vacationing canoeist can experience several streams without traveling very far. This is also true when canoeing the Pine; the Manistee, which it feeds, and the Pere Marquette, a bit south in Lake and Mason counties, can be experienced in a three-day weekend.

Note: There is another Pine River, which flows for 110 miles through Isabella, Montcalm, Gratiot, and Midland counties before joining the Tittabawassee River near the town of Midland. The put-in point is near Remis, and once afloat you will find the stream shallow and weedy. There are also several portages around dams.

Pere Marquette River

For a hundred miles the Pere Marquette River is a fast trout water with many quick turns along its wooded course.

For tackle-busting trout, the Pere Marquette is your river. Though the average depth is three feet, forest trees lean over the banks in places to shade fifteen-foot-deep pools. Below Walhalla anglers leave enough tackle festooned on stumps, logs, and the river bottom, lost to strong trout, to stock a fishing tackle shop. This is not a leisurely stream, and the canoeist must be ever vigilant for overhanging or fallen trees, log jams, and changing courses.

Running rapids on Michigan rivers is relatively safe because of their shallow depth.

Access is southeast of Baldwin or at the Route 37 bridge south of Baldwin. Another put-in point is at Bowman bridge, about five miles west of Baldwin via Carrs Road. Rainbow Rapids, an hour or so below the Bowman bridge, should be portaged on the south (port) side if, after looking over the rapids, you decide you do not want to shoot them. If you do shoot the Rainbow, be prepared for a series of four fast rips. Take the first three along the left shore and then make a right angle turn—very quickly—and ferrying if you must, drive your canoe to the right bank for the run through the final rip. Below Walhalla there are fewer snags, and upon approach to Pere Marquette Lake at Ludington the river separates in a delta-like series of many channels through mud flats. In season, be prepared with mosquito repellent.

There are many camping places along the entire course, and the river water is potable. The Ludington Chamber of Commerce can arrange pick-up service. Canoes and supplies are available at the small towns en route: Baldwin, Branch, Custer, and Scottville, all a short hike north of the river.

Big South Branch, Pere Marquette River

This branch of the Pere Marquette is included here for those who may wish to forgo canoeing the nearby crowded Manistee, Pine, or Pere Marquette rivers. The advantages include a quiet, leisurely trip with little or no fast water. The log jams pose little problem in the soft current.

This trip is ideally taken in several stages: Start first at 13-mile road about five miles west of Bitely, in Newaygo County. You will cruise along oak hardwood hills and through some cedar swamps to the Huntley bridge, near the Oceana County line. You can take out here or go downstream on an all-day trip to a public access site about eight miles south of Walhalla. Your progress will be slowed by log jams along the way, but the good brown trout fishing will compensate. Neither "No trespassing" nor "Keep off the grass" signs intrude on this river, as most of the land is publicly owned.

Big Sable River

The Sable River, in Lake and Mason counties, runs through Big Bear Swamp and through a tangle of backwoods in an undefiled course to Hamlin Lake. The canoeist can see deer with their heads completely submerged feeding on underwater vegetation and heron rookeries that date back farther than present-day residents can remember. Pike fishing in the undercut banks is possible. You cannot hurry this trip, which is an antidote to our modern-day pace. After the put-in at Route 669 bridge in Lake County, it is thirty-five miles to Upper Hamlin Lake, north of Ludington.

Muskegon River

This river rises in Higgins and Houghton lakes in Roscommon County and flows southwesterly for 227 miles to its terminus at Lake Michigan. It drains a watershed approximately 2 miles wide and 121 miles long. Except for the stretch between Hersey and Newaygo, where the drop is 4.4 feet per mile, giving rise to some fast rips, the Muskegon is a mild-tempered river. The upper half of the river is especially delightful.

After the put-in at Houghton Lake on the west shore, where the river rises, you will thread through Deadstream Swamp above Reedsburg dam. There is a good campground at Evart, but one should be wary of the rocks before reaching it. You can take on supplies at this town on Route 10.

The next stretch, to Hersey, is twelve miles of prime smallmouth bass water. At Big Rapids there is a campsite on the east side of the pond. From Big Rapids to Rogers dam there are thirteen miles of bass and northern pike fishing. Canoeists should portage the dam on the right side. The next dam is Hardy, sixteen miles away, and the portage takeout is on the west side of the dam. Below Hardy, you enter the heavily wooded Croton dam backwater, which offers fishing for bass, northern pike, walleye, and rainbow trout. The portage takeout at Croton is on the right side, and in the thirteen-mile stretch to Newaygo the trout fishing improves.

From Newaygo to Bridgeton is thirteen miles of good smallmouth bass fishing, high banks and lowlands, some farms along the way, and camping spots. On the final stretch the Muskegon slows down and there is more farmland and a swampy area as you paddle on to the town of Muskegon, where the river meets Lake Michigan.

Au Sable River

This sinuous river, with its water singing over pebbles and rocks and no dangerous rapids, is the most popular and most canoed river in Michigan and probably in the United States. The riverbank scenery is beautifully laid open with each passing mile. Along the river's wilder stretches deer come out on the sandbars to drink, and in the evening they can be observed in the meadows. The entire river, from Grayling to Lake Huron, is 180 miles, but the first seventy-five miles offer the best canoeing water.

To eliminate the congestion at Grayling, where about 3,000 rental canoes are available from the several liveries there, begin your trip at the Wakely bridge, about twenty-five miles downstream. Rentals and pickup are available. The south branch enters the main stream a short distance below this bridge. If you think you would enjoy cruising both rivers, begin on this branch first. Take-in is off Route 27 south of Grayling, at Stekert or Chase bridge. The water is about the same as in the main stream, the scenery is very interesting, there are no dangerous rapids, and the fishing is recommended. Canoeists should figure on two days for this trip.

On the main stream again, McMaster Bridge is about fifteen miles downstream. It is another nine miles to the Parmalle bridge, nine more miles to the Camp 10 bridge, and then the dam at Mio is but four miles away. In the big backwater stay close to the shore if the wind is strong. On occasion the waves run high on a windy day. There is a good campsite here, and takeout for finishing your Au Sable trip is highly recommended. Below Mio the water is slow, and there are six hydrodams to portage—all of which would take the edge off the pleasant memories of Au Sable's first seventy-five magnificant miles.

A CANOE COMPANY-SPONSORED TRIP. The Sawyer Canoe Company,* based at Oscoda, offers a unique canoe trip package: rental of their canoes for trips of three hours to seven days. The short trip of eighteen miles is the most popular and offers a shakedown cruise, an introduction to canoeing for couples, families, and groups. The current below the Foote Site dam runs slightly faster than four miles per hour, enabling you to make the eighteen-mile trip with little effort in about three hours. There are no rapids, waterfalls, log jams, or other such hazards in the river, and neither are there houses, buildings, or clusters of people along the route. You get the feeling that you are exploring a back-in-the-bush river.

After you park your car in the company parking lot, your party and equipment are transported upstream for as long a trip as you wish. Your trip will terminate at your car, where you started, and you will not have to wait for a pickup. You are not confined to a definite deadline for pickup, so you can set your own pace: paddling, fishing, swimming, taking side trips for fishing, or hiking the forest trails and enjoying a peaceful return to nature.

Tittibawassee River

The historic waters of the Tittibawassee, winding through a forest hinterland, offer the experience of floating the Indian and logger's water highway of an earlier day. Numerous tributaries and inlets offer exploration possibilities in side excursions. Placid vistas can be seen over low banks, and at times the river races between sheer banks twenty to thirty feet high to offer exciting visual contrasts as well as paddling action.

Put-in is on the upper reaches of either the main stream

---

*For details, contact Sawyer Canoe Company, P.O. Box 104, Oscoda, Michigan 48750.

or the east branch, about fifteen miles northeast of Gladwin at Route 61. There are several campsites available, and supplies are available at Gladwin and Beaverton. The take-out is at either Wixom Lake or the Edenville dam.

Shiawassee River

Shiawassee is the name of a county, a small town, and the river that flows for sixty-five miles through Oakland, Gene-see, Shiawassee, and Saginaw counties in the southern section of the lower peninsula. The Shiawassee is a peace-ful stream that meanders through agricultural country. The put-in point is at Holly at Route 75 or at anyone of the bridges downstream. Due to the numerous rocky riffles, especially below Owosso, the best time to canoe this stream is before June or after the fall rains. Picnic sites are available. There are dams at Byron, Shiawassee, Corunna, and Owosso, but the portaging of them presents no problem.

Some interesting historical sites include the first trading post in Shiawassee County at Knaggstown; the site of an early Indian reservation; old Indian gardens where Webb Creek joins the Shiawassee; and the birthplace of Thomas Dewey in Owosso.

Grand River

Add the Grand River, which rambles for 185 miles in scenic beauty through seven counties, to your collection, and you will be able to boast of the experience of canoeing the most crooked river in Michigan. The river also meanders through four cities—Jackson, Lansing, Grand Rapids, and Grand Haven—before it enters Lake Michigan. There are numerous dams along the river's 185-mile course, but there is little fishing water. To make the trip worthwhile, the Grand runs through a beautiful valley, revealing a continu-ously unfolding riverine tableau.

In canoeing the Grand it is best to divide it into convenient short trips, eliminating passage through the cities. Parnell Road, two miles north of Jackson, is a recommended starting point. Your first camping area will be about twenty-five miles away. Under no circumstances should the river water be used for drinking or cooking. Get water from farms along the way, in towns, at nearby homes, or at gas stations.

The adequate put-in and takeout points at the many bridges en route facilitate the bypassing of Lansing and Grand Rapids with their congestion, dams, and so on. The final stretch is through scenic farm country from Grandville to Grand Haven. Below Eastmanville is probably the only part of the river where fishers should string their lines. At Grand Haven you can take out in the town proper or paddle down to Lake Michigan and Grand Haven State Park, where there is a good campsite.

Kalamazoo River

The portion of this river that offers the best canoeing experience is from Allegan (Routes 89 and 40) to Saugatuck. There are well-developed state forest campgrounds in the county and numerous other places along the bank for unrestricted camping. The river flows between high banks and forests with many large trees.

A popular put-in point is at Echo Point, two miles northwest of Allegan on Monroe Road. You will then paddle three miles on Allegan Lake before taking out east of the dam for portage to a put-in site on the downstream side. The next stretch of river takes you along the Swan Creek Wildlife Refuge, a spring and fall resting place for thousands of migratory ducks and Canada geese. After reaching the Route 89 bridge, a possible takeout, there are seven miles of open stream, including a canoe camping site one and one-half miles below the bridge. To finish the trip, take out any place along the right bank at Saugatuck, unless you wish to continue through to Lake Michigan and down to the

Saugatuck beach, which through the years has been a young person's rendezvous.

St. Joseph River

This southwestern river is born at Sturgeon Lake near Colon at Route 86, where you can put in. You will meander over a lot of Indian trail water as you cruise this river, which flows through agricultural country. Most of the camping places along the shore are on private property, and canoeists need to get the owner's permission to spend the night. At the same time, they should ask about fruit, milk, or other farm products for sale.

After a lift-over at the dam at Mendon, your next stop will be Sturgis. En route, you will pass under a covered bridge, a rare experience in Michigan. Take out on the left side at the Sturgis dam, not to be confused with the city of Sturgis, which is south of the dam. There is both fast and slow water with plenty of photogenic scenery along the way to Three Rivers. The parks in the town deserve a stop, as a lot of history is associated with the region. The Chamber of Commerce will inform you about the historical and scenic areas to visit.

Beyond the dams at Three Rivers, Constantine and Mottville end this segment of the St. Joseph. The river turns southward and traverses the industrial complexes of this area in northern Indiana. After takeout and hauling canoes, passengers, and gear, the trip can be resumed at Niles or Berrien Springs for the final stretch to Benton Harbor or St. Joseph.

Huron River

This 100-mile river* flows through an extensive arc through

---

*For complete information on this river, write for the free *Huron River Canoeing Guides* from Huron-Clinton Metropolitan Authority, 1750 Guardian Bldg., Detroit, Michigan 48226.

Milford and Ann Arbor and to the south of Detroit, where it empties into Lake Erie.

INFORMATION SOURCES

"Canoeing in Michigan" is available from the Michigan Department of Natural Resources, Lansing, Michigan 48909. The guide is sketchy, but it supersedes previous guides.

"Let's Go Canoeing" is available from the Recreational Canoeing Association, Box 265, Baldwin, Michigan 49304. It offers information on canoe trips.

"Grand River Tributary Canoeing Maps" for the Maple, Flat, Red Cedar, Thornapple, Portage and Upper Grand, Rouge, and Flat rivers are available from the Michigan Grand River Watershed Council, 3322 West Michigan Avenue, Lansing, Michigan 48917.

6
Adventure Trails of Minnesota

Minnesota offers an interesting landscape, from rich, rolling farmland in the south and the prairie land in the west to cutover forests among the lakes and rivers in the north.

Minnesota was originally inhabited by the Chippewas and the Sioux, and for two centuries there was a constant struggle for the bountiful lands of the state. The Chippewa, of Algonquin stock, were mentioned by the explorer Nicolet as early as 1634. The first whites to enter the region were the explorers Radisson and Groseilliers, who came around 1659. They were followed by Duluth in 1679; Father Hennepin, who discovered and named the Falls of St. Anthony in 1680; and Perrot, who erected Fort Frontenac on Lake Pepin (part of the Mississippi River) in 1686.

Through the Treaty of Paris (1763), the French ceded the region of modern Minnesota east of the Mississippi to England, and twenty years later it became a part of the United States. The portion west of the Mississippi was acquired as part of the Louisiana Purchase (1803).

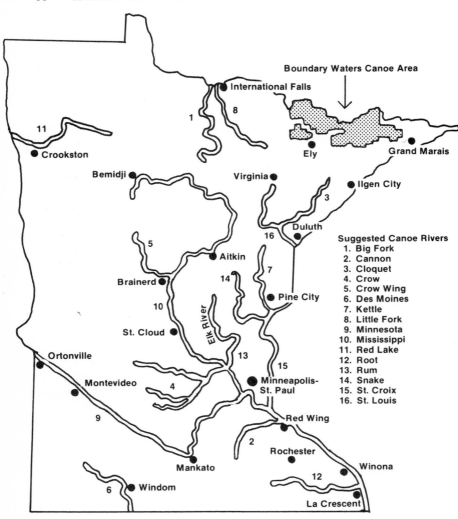

These canoe trails were designated by legislative action, which resulted from a special study report entitled, "Recreational Study of Rivers of Minnesota," compiled by Midwest Planning for the Conservation Department.

Minnesota Canoe Trails

The state of 15,291 lakes (though its auto license plate boasts but 10,000) claims more fresh water than any state in the union. In addition, there are 1,900 miles of trout streams and 13,100 miles of other inland rivers. At Itasca State Park several springs converge and give birth to a lilting small stream that meanders for 2,550 miles to the Gulf of Mexico—the Mississippi River.

When Hernando DeSoto, the first foreigner to record his arrival, reached the Mississippi in 1541, the mighty river was already a prized resource and an important artery for Indian travelers and warriors. Its banks were the site of, in turn, Indian villages, military forts, fur-trading posts, and ox-cart trails. Along with its ramified and pulsing tributaries, the Mississippi conveyed the canoes that carried the explorers to open up much of the Midwest. To this day the "Father of Waters" remains an important channel of commerce and recreation.

Minnesota, the "Land of Sky Blue Waters," does much to promote and support canoeing. Information is available in which the state's trails are described, routes recommended, accesses delineated, mileages indicated, and campsites and points of interest specified. In short, the state is a canoeist's dream come true.

As an aid to cruising canoeists, mileposts have been erected on the riverbanks and will be used in the text to designate highway bridges, access points, portages, historical sites, and other information deemed important and interesting to a successful trip.

Boundary Waters Canoe Area (BWCA)

Since 1909, when the Canadian portion of this was set aside as Quetico Provincial Park and the U.S. area as the Superior National Forest, the two countries have cooperated to preserve the inseparable unit of interlacing waterways as it has been from the days of antiquity. Originally, the combined area was known as Superior–Quetico Canoe Country, but now it is called the Boundary Waters Canoe Area (BWCA).

A canoe trail that is 318 years old, traveled by Radisson and Groseilliers in 1660, flows in this Shangri-la of canoeing waters, the greatest canoe country in the world. It is claimed to be the last true wilderness of the nation, with hundreds of lakes and connecting streams in deep forest marked only by old trails. This vast wilderness of 14,500 square miles of unspoiled land, of which 400,000 acres is virgin forest, is most popular with stateside canoeists, as the approximately 108,000 who annually ply its waters will attest.

Canoeists of all ages—from gray-haired couples to infants in arms, church and scout groups, high schoolers, college fraternities, foreigners, and socialites—take off from three main gateways: Grand Marais, Ely, and Crane Lake. Outfitting is available from all three to insure an exciting canoe trip, whether it be for days, weeks, or months. So extensive are the water trail possibilities that there is no need for backtracking. The land is relatively unchanged since the days of the 18th-century fur brigades, when French voyagers paddled their *canot de maitre* birchbarks and kept time to the boisterous singing of the steersman.

On and near BWCA waters modern canoeists can paddle,

Contestants paddle day and night in the annual canoe race from Ely, Minnesota, to Atikoken, Canada, to celebrate Independence Day and Canada's Dominion Day.

portage, and camp in the spirit of early French voyagers in a water and wood country where the canoe is still the only practical means of summer transportation. Canoeing is enjoyed from May through October. If at all possible, select the early and late days of the season; the waterways and campsites are less crowded, the fishing is better, and the insect pests are minimized.

A travel permit is required and is available free of charge from any Superior National Forest Office or, if more convenient, from your take-in point outfitter or resort. No reservations are required; campsites are filled on a first-come, first-serve basis. Once afloat, you will probably meander in and out of the Canadian sector. For crossing the international boundary, Canada maintains stations on three boundary lakes. The U.S. has custom offices in Ely, Crane Lake, and Grand Marais. Check with both the Canadian and U.S. offices when crossing over by canoe. Firearms are not permitted in the adjoining Canadian Quetico Provincial Park. They are not restricted in the BWCA, but they are discouraged. Fishing licenses are required. One party of up to fifteen persons is permitted on a campsite, and the stay is limited to two weeks. Pets are permitted, but they must be kept under control at all times. At the end of your BWCA visit, you must take out all nonburnable refuse such as empty cans, tinfoil, bottles, and so on. Litter bags are furnished by outfitters, and one is issued with each travel permit.

The outfitter is synonymous with canoeing the BWCA. You can choose the complete rental package: canoe, tent, food, packs, utensils, sleeping bag, air mattress, insect repellent, and so on. If you opt for this plan, you can be certain that the logistics of your trip are sound. In fact, even if you bring your own canoe, food, and gear, the outfitter is still an excellent source for on-the-spot, up-to-date information. Also, items such as a waterproof map, film, last-minute footstuffs, and so on can be obtained before taking off to the hinterland.

Maps* are furnished by outfitters, but should you wish some pretrip figuring, you will want maps beforehand. Perusing maps is an interesting wintertime activity.

The two best sources of information on entry into the BWCA, outfitting, and so on are the Chamber of Commerce, Ely, Minnesota, and Commercial Club, Crane Lake, Minnesota. Two other information sources are the Arrowhead Association, Duluth, Minnesota 55801, and the forest supervisor, Superior National Forest, Box 338, Duluth, Minnesota 55801.

Now, the bad news: Overuse is one of the greatest problems facing the BWCA today. This is profoundly true of the traditional Moose Lake, Fall Lake, and Lake One points of entry. U.S. Forest officials project that a saturation point will be reached soon and that a "user distribution program" must be put into operation. This would help alleviate the problem, insure a better distribution of users, and ultimately limit the number allowed to enter the area.

Next, the good news: As with population in general, the problem is not that there are too many people, but that they tend to concentrate in tight, small areas. A canoe wilderness of 14,500 square miles can handle every canoeist intent on a trip there. Quite simply, the entry portals to the vast interior must be increased. Robert Beymer has indicated that a start has already been made in that direction. In his article "Another Way into the BWCA,"** he personally discovers eight alternative entries to BWCA waters.

---

*A complete atlas of the entire BWCA can be purchased from W. A. Fisher Co., Virginia, Minnesota 55792. The map "Superior National Forest and the Boundary Waters Canoe Area" is available from the U.S. Forest Service, 710 N. 6th St., Milwaukee, Wisconsin. Contour maps of the BWCA are available at a small cost from the U.S. Geological Survey, Denver, Colorado 80225.

**Robert Beymer, "Another Way into the BWCA," *Canoe*, June 1976. Copies of his descriptions are available from the American Canoe Association, 4620 E. Evans Ave., Denver, Colorado 80222.

Big Fork River

The Big Fork* journeys for 173 miles and several hundred years back into the past. The route was used by Indians, fur traders, loggers, missionaries, and early settlers, who, as do modern canoeists, must have enjoyed its natural wonders: stately pines, massive hardwoods, somber spruce, fragrant balsam, vast fields of wild rice, furbearing animals, waterfowl, and moose—a rare stateside view these days.

MILE 173   Put-in is at County Route 29 bridge, Dora Lake Lodge and campsites are available.

MILE 152.7   Huck's Rapids access is from County Route 14, and four miles below is the privately owned Tippe-Canoe campsite, complete with water, tentsite, fireplace, and tables.

MILE 148.2   Bill Hafeman lives and works in his modest workshop here, which is aromatic with the smell of cedar and spruce shavings. Hafeman's birchbark canoe shop is located on the south bank of the Big Fork. This venerable craftsman builds birchbark canoes, and many feel that they are an improvement on the original Indian creations. Hafeman claims that all that is needed to build a Chippewa style "longnose" canoe are axe, awl, knife, and materials found in the woods. Although the following steps are not necessarily listed sequentially, they will give you some idea of the care Hafeman takes with his creations. The outer skin is local birchbark cut from a healthy tree and soaked in water. The cedar ribs, hand-trimmed with a knife, are steamed and placed over forms to give the canoe the desired shape. The cedar strips for the bow construction are

---

*Information is available from the district foresters at Effice, Big Falls, and Loman. John Helgerson at Scenic State Park, Bigfork, and Arthur Enis at Big Falls are other good sources.

lashed together with a binding of spruce roots that are split and peeled of bark. Cedar-strip planking is also hand-split and trimmed to proper dimensions. The gunwales are attached with the spruce root lashing. All holes are made with an awl, not drilled, and neither nails nor screws are used. Asphalt, for caulking the birchbark joints, is the only modern material used. It is a substitute for the original spruce gum, which softens in hot weather and requires much maintenance.

Examples of Hafeman's canoes can be observed at the Superior National Forest visitor center in Ely; another is enshrined at the Minnesota Historical Society. If you cannot drop in on Hafeman via the water route, you can drive in via Route 6. His canoe shop is found just before you cross the river, about fifty miles north of Grand Rapids.

A finished birchbark canoe, hand-crafted from local materials found in the woods.

MILE 130.3   This historic site, Klondike Landing, is privately owned and has fresh water, picnic tables, and so on.

MILE 125 There is an excellent access from Route 1 to a roadside park with tables, toilets, and trash cans but no water. Less than a mile down is Busties's Landing, which was named for the Indian Chief Bustie.

MILE 106.8 A portage is mandatory on the left side of Little American Falls.

MILE 106.2 TO 97.6 There are six accesses to the river via both county and forest service roads.

MILE 76.3 Mondo Campground offers complete facilities and in addition there is a hiking trail along an old logging road. Access is from Route 6.

MILE 56 Trout fishing in the feeder streams is available.

MILE 53 Portage is necessary because of the Big Falls Rural Electrification Administration hydroelectric plant. There is a municipal park and campgrounds with tables, fireplaces, and toilet. Access is via Route 13.

MILE 42.6 Ben Lynn Landing and campground has tables, fireplaces, and toilet. The access if via Route 13.

MILE 30.2 This is the site of the Hudson Bay Trading Post and Indian portage.

MILE 30 Keuffner's Landing is a possible takeout point at Route 3.

MILE 19.4 Another possible takeout is at Lindford Bridge Landing at Route 1.

MILE 9.5 Bear River, Route 10, provides still another takeout point.

MILE 9   A final takeout point is at Minnesota Route 11 bridge. Please note that in the final thirty miles there are four takeout points for consideration.

Crow Wing River

The Crow Wing* is probably the most ideal family cruising river in the Moccasin Flower State. There are only two dams with short carryovers and lots of safe swimming in water that is so clear you can count the pebbles on the bottom. The consistently moderate current makes possible a relaxing cruise in a semiwild atmosphere that can be enjoyed even with small children. En route are ample campsites with sanitary facilities, and there are activity possibilities for all members of the family.

The Crow Wing River begins in a chain of lakes and flows south to the Mississippi River. In the twenty-five miles from milepost 91 to milepost 66, there are seven bridges over the river and two campsites. Proceeding downstream, the following mileposts are significant:

MILE 57.7   Anderson's Crossing has a campsite, old Indian crossing, and a pioneer homestead.

MILE 54.5   This is the site of Funk's landing and campsite.

MILE 41.9   Knob Hill Campsite has 105 acres.

MILE 39   Swimming and picnicking is available at Cottingham County Park.

MILE 33.4   Bullard Bluff, an eighty-acre campsite, is the site of Indian mounds and a crossing.

---

*Resource is Crow Wing Trail Association, Box 210, Sebeka, Minnesota 56477. Supplies are available at Huntersville and Oylen. Outfitters include Ed Patson at Menahga, Irv Funk at Nimrod, Bob's Marina at Wadena, and Turk Kennelly at Menahga.

MILE 30   This is the site of Old Wadena Fort and the confluence of the Partridge River.

MILE 28.5   McGivern Park has forty acres complete with rifle range and shelters for picnicking.

MILE 16.4   The Route 10 bridge at Motley offers a takeout point for those who decide against reaching the Mississippi River, which would entail a dam and a portage at mile 8.7 and at mile 3.3.

Kettle River

The Kettle River* (53 miles) is especially interesting because of its ever-changing shoreline. It is rich in lumbering history of the 1850s and '60s when the logs came floating down and the chanteys of the lumberjacks were heard. Today shy wildlife, the songs of birds, and the splash of rising fish blend with the sounds of the woods to help make a satisfying canoe trip. Although there are no campsites on the river, four developed access points make it ideal for day trips. Only the Upper Kettle is extremely wild, with a two-mile chute of fast water, and only the experienced canoeist should challenge this stretch.

MILE 51   Begin your trip at County Route 12 bridge. The access is on the southeast corner of the bridge.

MILE 42.5   A two-mile stretch of scenic, dense hardwood forest and braided stream can pose problems because of the low trees and twisting nature of the main current.

MILE 40.3   Here is the confluence of the Moose River. A

---

*Information sources include the district forester at Hinckley; Ron Bergum, Soil Conservation Service, Hinckley; the Apco Station at Moose Lake; and the Standard, Texaco, Mobil, and Phillips gas stations at the Hinckley intersection of Routes 48 and 35.

short distance downstream is a small scenic campsite set in a stand of large conifers on the right (east) bank.

MILE 32.2   County Route 33 bridge has a developed access and parking on the southeast corner. Supplies are available at the town of Rutledge, located one block west.

MILE 29.4   Short, heavy rapids are experienced here. A scenic campsite is available on the rock outcrop ten feet above the river on the west bank.

MILE 25.7   A takeout point of many canoeists is at the State Route 23 bridge, which has a developed access, parking, and a gravel launching ramp on the northeast corner. *Caution*: Takeout is advised here, because below are the very impressive Dalles of the Kettle River and Hell's Gate Rapids, which are tricky and dangerous and which have taken the lives of three canoeists in the past several years.

MILE 20   Kettle River dam is a good place to reenter the river. Parking, a picnic area, and river access are available.

MILE 19.2   There are three short but heavy rapids located here. The river downstream toward State Route 48 may throw standing waves.

MILE 12.4   Route 48 offers access, parking, picnic tables, and a gravel launching ramp provided by the Hinckley Sportsmen Club. This is another recommended takeout. The remainder of the trip to the confluence of the St. Croix River, twelve more miles, is a fast, rock-dodging run in high water, and there is a very long portage in low water.

Little Fork River

The Little Fork* (123 miles) offers the sights of moose in

---

*Information sources include the district forester at International Falls, the area forester at Little Fork, and the conservation officer at Cook.

the muskeg swamps, of deer browsing in the open meadows, of bear in the woods, and beaver, muskrat, and waterfowl along the feeder streams. The fishing is for muskie and walleye pike. Thus, with moose, beaver, and muskies, the river qualifies for rating as a wild stream.

MILE 132.2 The trip begins at the town of Cook. The terrain is rolling farmland. The access is at the southeast corner of the Route 53 bridge.

MILE 118 There is a wayside park with access on the southwest corner of the Route 73 bridge.

MILE 116 Hananen's Falls and Rapids is a scenic area that requires a portage on the south bank. There are campsites on the portage. Below this point the river has intermittent rapids, some of which must be run with extreme care and only under normal water conditions. There are recurrent rapids for the next twelve miles. The small falls at mile 97.3 may be run only in high water.

MILE 94.4 There is access from the northeast corner under the Silverdale bridge at State Route 65. There is an excellent campsite, and canoes can be rented at Silverdale Tavern. There is good muskie and walleye fishing for the next forty miles, or up to the Route 65 bridge.

MILE 90.8 A campsite is located on the south bank of the LeVallee River confluence, where canoeists can spend the night fishing the LeVallee for brown trout.

MILE 87 This is the beginning of the Nett Rapids; one-half mile farther is the Net Lake Indian Reservation boundary line.

MILE 70.8 Seller Rapids, the roughest rapids on the entire trip, are located here. They are rougher than the Deadman's Rapids, eight miles downstream, which are not as difficult as the name implies. The Flat Rock campsite or lunch spot is located between these two rapids.

MILES 53.9, 51, AND 37.8   Campsites are available at these mileposts.

MILE 28   Flat Rock Rapids offer access, a campsite, and a popular spot to swim and picnic.

MILE 23.1   Access and campsite are available at Ed John's sawmill.

MILE 21.9   The lower rapids are found at this milepost.

MILE 19.9   The Route 219 bridge has rapids underneath.

MILE 15   It is possible to take out at the Route 71 bridge on the northwest corner, where there is a campsite, or one can finish the trip fifteen miles downstream, at the confluence of the Rainy River. Takeout is on the northeast bank at the end of the trip.

Minnesota River

The Minnesota River,* flowing through granite outcroppings and heavily forested banks for several hundred miles, is rich in natural and human history. Exploration of this watershed dates back to the mid-1600s, when French explorers reached the river on their way west. On the river's long route to the Mississippi River its drop is less than one foot per mile, which eliminates rapids, falls, and the need for portages. The river has many bridges providing put-in and takeout locations, so a trip may be planned to suit one's fancy.

The headwaters of the Minnesota River rise in Brown's

---

*Information sources include the Division of Game and Fish, Mankato; the Chambers of Commerce at New Ulm and at Redwood Falls, and Big Stone Lake State Park at Ortonville.

Valley on the Minnesota–South Dakota border. Leaving Stone Lake, the river begins its 330-mile flow to join the Mississippi. The lower part of the river has a drop of less than one foot per mile as it flows through a wide and deep valley.

MILE 289   Canoeists should start at Big Stone Lake in Ortonville, at the southeast corner of the Route 30 bridge. A short portage on the right is necessary early in the trip because of the big stone dam. From here to Marsh Lake (Mile 271) trees and vines intermesh over the river to give a junglelike effect; dark-shaded woods of maple, cottonwood, and elm fringe the banks. There are some snags, which require one to chop through or carry over or around. Some broken-down bridges also create obstacles.

MILE 266.6   Marsh Lake dam, located here, has a total of five access points on the lake proper.

MILES 252 TO 264   Six access points, four state owned, one federal, and one private, are found at Lac qui Parle Lake located here.

MILE 239.4   At Montevideo the Camp Release State Historical Wayside Park is found. This is the site of the Sioux uprising of 1862, which began in the Minnesota Valley and resulted in the death of about 450 settlers and an unknown number of Indians.

MILE 224.6   This is the beginning of granite outcrops and small rapids just above Granite Falls, which is one mile downstream. The dam for the hydroelectric station is also here. The river channel is 100 to 150 feet wide here. The dam at Granite Falls should be portaged for about sixty yards on the south bank. About two miles below the falls on the way to Minnesota Falls, canoeists find minor rapids and a pool.

MILE 220.6   Minnesota Falls, a dam, a historic townsite

and Catfish Haven Resort are located at this milepost. Canoeists should portage on the right.

MILE 203.9   Joseph R. Brown state historical wayside park is located one-fourth mile off the river on the north bank at this milepost.

MILE 197.6   Granite ridges, cedars, and small lakes make this milepost a scenic area.

MILE 195.2   Schwandt State Monument is located in this picturesque area, as is a historic gold mine.

MILE 188.9   Camp Pope, a historic site, is found at this milepost. For the next fifty-five miles, several more historic sites are situated along the river.

MILE 134.7   There is a wayside park off Route 14.

MILE 102.2   Sibley Park, located here, has access and parking.

MILE 100.5   This is the site of the hanging of Indian insurgents in 1863.

MILE 85.6   This is the location of historic St. Peter. Access and a campsite is found on the southwest corner of Route 99 bridge in the city park.

MILE 79.9   Ottowa Ghost Town makes this an interesting milepost.

MILE 66   Joe Brown House in historic Henderson is here. Access is on the southeast corner of Route 19.

MILE 35.8   Carver Rapids, Indian mounds, and a trading post site are all found here.

MILE 32   Historic Carver is located here.

MILE 29.7   Chaska is a possible takeout at the Route 41 bridge, or if one prefers, one could take out four miles downstream at Shakopee at the Route 169 bridge.

Mississippi River

Before flowing out of the state, the Mississippi* passes through parts of ten counties, covering about 600 miles. Many one- or two-day trips may be taken along its ever-changing course; canoes can be launched at the many town, state, and federal campsites or where a bridge crosses over the water trail. Canoeists can select the cruise that suits their taste and engage in such diverse and exciting activities as picnicking, swimming, fishing, or shooting rapids. They can also observe nature, geology, or historical sites, and always in the background there is a natural scenic vista.

This section will rather sketchily review the upper 430 miles of the Mississippi—from its origin in the bubbling springs at Itasca State Park to its confluence with the Rum River.

MILE 430   Itasca State Park—the beginning milepost—is visited by nearly a million visitors each year. This is where the 2,552-mile Mississippi River is born.

MILE 425   Here can be found Wanagan Landing, access, a picnic area, and a campsite. For the next sixty miles the river varies from large marsh to cool pine-lined corridors, but this portion of the river is for the most part just as it was when Henry Schoolcraft discovered the source of the Mississippi in 1832.

MILE 422.5   This is the location of Vekin's Dam. Portage is

---

*Information sources include the Minnesota State Forestry Station at Itasca State Park and the Division of Lands and Forestry stations at Bemidji, Guthrie, and Itasca.

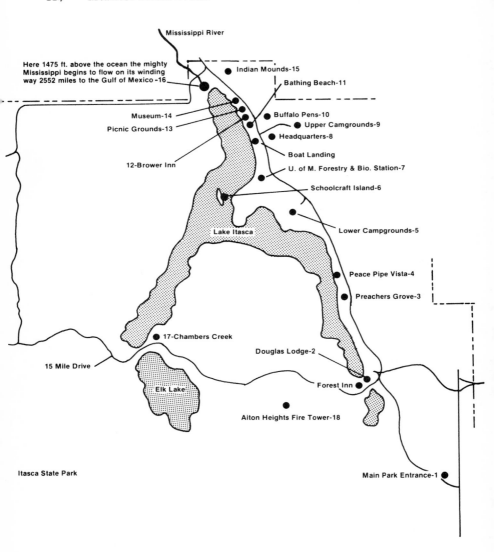

Mississippi River

Here 1475 ft. above the ocean the mighty
Mississippi begins to flow on its winding
way 2552 miles to the Gulf of Mexico –16

Indian Mounds-15

Bathing Beach-11

Museum-14

Picnic Grounds-13

Buffalo Pens-10

Upper Camgrounds-9

Headquarters-8

Boat Landing

12-Brower Inn

U. of M. Forestry & Bio. Station-7

Schoolcraft Island-6

Lake Itasca

Lower Campgrounds-5

Peace Pipe Vista-4

Preachers Grove-3

17-Chambers Creek

Douglas Lodge-2

15 Mile Drive

Elk Lake

Forest Inn

Aiton Heights Fire Tower-18

Itasca State Park

Main Park Entrance-1

Itasca State Park.

necessary for 25 yards on the left.

MILE 421.4   There are rapids under the bridge at County Route 37.

MILE 413.1   Coffee Pot Landing, access, campsite, picnic area, and a footbridge crossing are found at this milepost.

MILE 405.9   Rapids are found at this milepost.

MILE 396.3   Bear Den Landing is located here, with access, campsite, and picnic area.

MILE 392.4   Found here is Pine Point Landing with access, campsites, and picnic area. Rice Lake is located to the north.

MILE 383.7   Iron Bridge campsite and picnic area, which is unaccessible by road, is found here.

MILE 373.4   County Route 11 bridge, Carr Lake, and Schoolcraft River bridge are all located here.

MILE 371.1   Lake Irving is found here.

MILE 370   Routes 2 and 71 in Bemidji are found at this milepost.

The next part of the Mississippi River* canoe route starts in Bemidji, which was named for Chief Bemidji, a Chippewa chief.

MILE 370   Put-in is at Lake Bemidji. Another put-in, perhaps better, is at the state park on the east shore about three miles away at the Route 19 bridge.

---

*Information sources are the district ranger, Cass Lake District, Chippewa National Forest, Cass Lake; the dam tender at Winnie Dam; and the U.S. Corps of Engineers office at Deer River. For the Grand Rapids area, Lee Gaalas of the Grand Rapids Division of Game and Fish at Brainerd and the area forester at Bemidji are good sources.

MILE 362.1 Canoeists must portage right for 150 yards at the Ottertail Power Company dam, located here.

MILE 355.2 Route 8 access is found here. This is also the boundary of the Chippewa National Forest and Old Red Lake Oxcart Trail.

MILE 350 Lake Windigo picnic area and Star Island campsite are both located at this milepost.

MILE 335.5 West Winnie campsite and access are found here.

MILE 325 At this milepost there are excellent side trips to four improved campsites: West Seelye Bay, East Seelye Bay, Masomo Point, and William Narrows.

MILE 321 Plug Hat Point, campsites, and access are found at this milepost.

MILE 320.9 At Lake Winnibigoshish (Winnie) Dam, located here, portage is to the right.

MILE 295 White Oak Point, site of an old Indian village and trading post in 1895, is the landmark at this milepost.

MILE 287.3 Campsites are available at the Schoolcraft State Park, located here.

MILE 276.3 Access is available at Cohasset found here.

MILE 274.4 At Pokegama dam portage is to the left. Early falls and rapids have been replaced by dams at this milepost and also at Grand Rapids. Located nearby is Pokegama Lake, which is thirteen miles long. However, it is not on the canoe route.

MILE 271.3   At the Blandin Paper Company dam portage is to the right. This is the early historic site of the Grants' Northwest Trading Post.

MILE 271   Grand Rapids, located here, has an access and is an excellent stopover to stretch the legs, buy supplies, and so on. It is the site of an early fur-trading post. The route for steamboats carrying passengers and freight was located downstream from Grand Rapids. Some steamboats operated well into the 20th century.

MILE 270   Legion Park, with campsite, is found at this milepost.

MILE 268   Prairie River and historic Guner's Landing are located here.

MILE 239   Historic Swan River Logging Camp is a landmark well worth visiting.

MILE 238   County Park campsite at the town of Jacobson, Routes 65 and 200, is a possible takeout point. It might be interesting to note that in 1894 the Steamer Fawn sank here.

   The next portion of the Mississippi* leads to Rum River. For eight miles (mile 236 to 228), there are five historic landings. They include Cox, Ferrose, Cut-off, Ball Bluff, and Pine Rapids. This portion of the river is rich in historical sites.

MILE 224   Crooked Rapids are located at this milepost.

MILE 223.8   Verdon Post Office Landing is the site where the steamboat Irene sank in 1908.

---

*Information is available at Fort Snelling State Park, St. Paul. See also earlier references.

Canoe race on the upper Mississippi River near Grand Rapids, sponsored by the Minnesota Canoe Association.

MILE 217.6   Noyes Rapids are featured at this milepost.

MILE 216.7   This is the historic site of Lee's Ferry, and two miles downstream is found Doney's and Scriver's landings.

MILE 212.4   Sandy Lake dam has campsites on both sides of the dam. It has an excellent access and is the site of the early Northwest Company Fur-Trading Post.

MILE 208.8   Sandy Lake Rapids are found here.

MILE 207.8 TO 179.9   There are thirteen historic sites to visit.

MILE 178   Control dam and Aitkin drainage ditch are found here.

MILE 172   A good access point is located here.

MILE 144.2   This is the historic site of the Chippewa encampment.

MILES 137 AND 125.5   There are wayside parks here and

also an access, at mile 137.

MILE 124.8   Portage is to the right for the dam located here.

MILE 113   This historic site of the abandoned town of Crow Wing is now Crow Wing State Park.

MILE 104.3   The historic Bates Trading House of 1831 is of interest here.

MILE 100.5   South of historic Fort Ripley, located here, is an area called "Painted Rocks" by the French voyagers. It served as the winter headquarters of Zebulon Pike during the winter of 1805–06 while Pike was searching for the source of the Mississippi.

MILE 88.9   Portage is to the left for the dam.

MILE 87.3   Charles Lindbergh State Park is located here.

MILE 80.5   Blanchard dam is the site of the Chippewa boundary of 1825.

MILES 58.3 AND 52.7   Portage is to the right for dams located at these markers.

MILE 53   A wayside park is available here.

MILE 12.7   A wayside park and campsites are welcome features here.

MILE 7.5   This is the site of a historic Indian trading post, a wayside park, and access.

MILE 0   A historic fur-trading post is found here, where

the Rum River enters the Mississippi River.

Root River

The Root River,* 82 miles long, is another family canoeing stream, becoming so after the spring runoff from melting snow. The towering, forested bluffs at the water's edge narrow the river to a tree-banked canyon, making it unique among canoeing rivers. Although the river itself is seldom over three feet deep, there are some deeper pools. There are no major waterfalls, but there are a number of rapids with large rocks rising above the rushing water.

MILE 82.4   The bridge on Route 5 at Chatfield provides the put-in site on the northwest side. From here the river flows easterly as a direct tributary to the Mississippi River. This upper section has a continuous change of scenery with just enough fast water and rapids to make a canoe trip challenging. There are many potential campsites with elevations high enough to catch the breezes and to keep insects at a minimum.

MILE 78   The bridge on Route 52 has rapids and an island below the bridge.

MILE 64.9   High cliffs of vertical limestone, dolomite, sandstone, and shale provide interesting scenery. Route 21 bridge has an access on the southeast.

MILE 54   A campsite is located here.

MILE 53.5   From the Route 250 bridge at Lanesboro through Rushford and on to Hokah, the cliffs tower as high as 450 to 500 feet.

---

*Information sources include the Division of Game and Fish, Lanesboro; the district forester at Caledonia; Leo Giethbrook at Chatfield; and Ray Bentdahl at Preston.

MILE 40.3 The wayside park located here has a flowing spring.

MILE 37.4 A bridge at Route 16 is found here.

MILE 35.9 A campsite is located here.

MILE 35.4 The old dam found here creates turbulent water.

MILE 33.9 At Rushford Bridge is a campsite provided by the Sportsmen Club. From here to the Mississippi River the river tends to flow directly, as there are levees and channel improvements along the way. These changes in flow have caused fast water, but they have also reduced the frequency of rapids and obstructions. Paddling down this heavily wooded portion with its high hills and valleys is happy canoeing.

MILE 24.5 This is the location of a wayside park.

MILE 19.9 This is the location of Houston bridge.

MILE 18 The south fork of the Root River confluence is at this mile marker.

MILE 12.6 Neither Mound Prairie bridge nor Hokah bridge, six miles downstream, has an access. Therefore it is best to take out at the Route 26 bridge at mile 3.4.

Rum River

The Rum River flows southerly for 140 miles as a tributary of the Mississippi River. The 67-mile trip here is from Route 95 in Princeton to the takeout at the Anoka County Fairgrounds. The Rum River presents a variety of experiences and visual observations. In the upper portions, especially above Cambridge, the canoeist dwells in an area where nature is unblemished and wildlife thrives.

MILE 69   Put-in is at the Wayside park, located just north of the Route 95 bridge in Princeton.

MILE 58.6   The bridge on Route 7 provides an access located at the northwest corner of Spencer Brook.

MILE 53.7   Access is at the southwest corner, West Point, at the bridge on Route 47.

MILE 49.8   Supplies are available at the small store located one-half mile north of the bridge on Route 65 at Walbo.

MILE 44.1   The bridge on Route 14 is located here.

MILE 36.6   The Cambridge city park at the bridge over Route 95 provides picnic facilities, rest rooms, and drinking water.

MILE 30.9   Isanti Brook, one-half mile downstream at the Route 5 bridge, provides access to the town of Isanti. The shorelines become heavily wooded with elm, oak, maple, and ash trees. Along with the fifty- to sixty-foot-wide channel, a northwoods atmosphere prevails, even though there is an increase in homes, camps, and cottages from here to the end of the route.

MILE 29.7   There is a unique island campsite located here.

MILE 23.8   The bridge at Route 10 is found here.

MILE 19.7   There is a bridge at Route 24. Portage is to the right for the rapids over the old dam. There is a park and a store in St. Francis, on the right bank.

MILE 14.1 The Route 22 bridge is found here.

MILE 9.1 At the Route 7 bridge, there is a possible take-out at the southeast corner.

MILE 8.2 A boy scout camp is found on the right.

MILE 2.0 The Anoka County Fairgrounds and county park are located on the west bank. Water, a boat ramp, and picnic facilities are available.

MILE 1.1 At Anoka dam, the backup of water widens the river to between 200 and 300 feet.

St. Croix River

The St. Croix* is one of the finest rivers in the United States (see Appendix 3, National Wild and Scenic River System). From the St. Croix State Forest to its junction with the Mississippi, the St. Croix is both a Minnesota and Wisconsin river, as they share its banks for 120 miles.

MILE 120.0 At Danbury, Wisconsin, the Yellow River access is good.

MILE 114.9 There is access at State Route 48 and a campsite on the northwest corner of Minnesota.

MILE 106.4 Clam River access is good on the Wisconsin side.

MILE 105.4 St. Croix State Park has public access and an

---

*Information sources include Taylor Falls Canoe Company, Taylor Falls, Minnesota; the district foresters, Markville, Minnesota; the area forester, Cambridge, Minnesota; St. Croix State Park, Hinckley, Minnesota; Wayne Golly at Hinckley, Minnesota; and Don Klande at Forest Lake, Minnesota.

excellent campground.

MILES 98–94   This is the beginning of Kettle River Rapids. Here the St. Croix divides into two parts and is joined by the Kettle River at the lower end of the rapids. Below the rapids the river varies from 300 to 1,200 feet in width. There is an average gradient of 1.2 feet per mile and a depth of two to ten feet.

MILE 97.8   The Head-of-the-Rapids offers a good landing. This stretch of water represents one of the finest safe areas of fast water within Minnesota. It is challenging and exciting but not dangerous.

MILE 96.9   There is a good pit landing on the Minnesota side.

Minnesota fast-water canoeists use the spray skirt cover that fits tightly around the waist to keep from shipping water. (Old Town Canoe Company, Old Town, Maine)

MILE 93.4   The Foot-of-the-Rapids offers a good landing on the Wisconsin side.

MILE 91.2 The north side of the Snake River ferry landing is good.

MILE 82.5 There is a good access on the Minnesota side at Stevens Creek.

MILE 81.1 This is the site of a historic Indian camp.

MILE 78.3 The Rush City access on the Minnesota side is good.

MILE 71.8 This is the location of a historic Chippewa village, the site of an 1855 battle.

MILE 70.0 Located here is the Sunrise River access and the site of the historic Sunrise cemetery.

MILE 62.0 Nevers dam has a good access and is also a historic site.

MILE 53.0 St. Croix Falls is the location of a wayside park and an access on the Wisconsin side.

MILE 52.8 There is good access at Taylor Falls.

MILE 51.7 Portage on the left bank, at the sixty-foot-high dam. Equipment can be carried through the streets of town and put in at the landing on the Minnesota side.

MILE 51.0 Taylor Falls wayside park and Muller Boat landing provide food, canoe rental, and excursion boat rides.

MILE 50.8 This is the site of the Upper Dells.

MILE 48.3 The Lower Dells of the St. Croix, where the river flows through a wider valley and splits into several channels and backwaters, are found here. At the lower end the St. Croix becomes Lake St. Croix, a large linear reservoir created by a large natural bar at its juncture with the Mississippi River.

MILE 41.5   This is the historic site of a famous Indian battle.

MILE 40.9   The line of cedars here marks the Indian boundary of 1835.

MILE 39.8   There is an excellent campsite on the island.

MILE 35.7   William O'Brien State Park has access and campsites.

MILE 34.0   Historic Marine-on-St. Croix has a private access off Route 95 that is excellent. It is located one-fourth mile north of town hall. This is the site of the first commercially productive sawmill, circa 1838, and for eighty years this was the center of the colorful backwoods lumberjacking industry.

MILE 31.5   There are campsites available on Cedar Island.

MILE 24.9   Historic Boomsite Park is set in a historic and scenic area.

MILE 11.0   There is a campsite on the sandbar at historic Afton.

MILE 1.4   There is a campsite on the sandbar.

MILE 0   Historic Point Douglas is located at the juncture with the Mississippi River. There are three public accesses, but parking is inadequate.

St. Louis River

A recently created ninety-mile canoe route along the St.

Louis River* runs from Forbes to Cloquet and includes twelve primitive campsites and seven access points. A local canoe trail has long been the dream of canoeists in the area; it was finally developed by the Department of Natural Resources (DNR) in cooperation with the Minnesota Power and Light Company. The picturesque river is bordered by jackpine, black spruce, and Norway pine in its upper regions. At the outset there are many riffles created by sand and gravel bars, offering a constant challenge. Deer, moose, grouse, and other game thrive in the bankside forest. Families that enjoy combining fishing with canoeing will enjoy paddling this river, which offers catfish, northern pike, and walleye.

MILE 88.4   Canoeists can put in at the campsite and access point furnished by the Ford Taconite Plant, which is located off Route 16 directly west of Route 53. Here the river begins to narrow and deepen.

MILE 84.3   Portage to the right for the dam. At the put-in below the dam, rapids predominate for about 100 yards because of the narrowness.

MILE 82.6   The bridge at Route 7 provides an access.

MILES 78.5 AND 77.8   DNR campsites can be found on the right side.

MILE 70.3   There is an access at the Route 27 bridge.

MILE 68.8   A DNR campsite is found on the left bank.

MILE 63.2   Access is found at the Route 436 bridge.

MILE 61.9   A DNR campsite is located on the right bank.

*Information sources include the Division of Game and Fish, Duluth, Minnesota; district forester, Cotton, Minnesota; Jay Cook State Park, Carlton, Minnesota; the conservation officer at Biwabik, Minnesota; Gerald McHugh at Virginia, Minnesota; Floyd Jaros at Cloquet, Minnesota; and Otto Leerson at Cloquet, Minnesota.

MILE 53.0   Access is found at the Route 52 bridge.

MILE 50.0   There is a DNR campsite on the left bank.

MILE 39.2   Here, at the site of the confluence of the White Face River, the St. Louis River widens to over 200 feet.

MILE 33.0   Floodwood city park, on the northeast corner off Route 8, is a historic site commemorating portage on east Savanna River. Supplies are available at Floodwood.

MILE 30.0   With the Boulder Field Rapids beginning here, this is a scenic area.

MILE 27.7   The severe rapids moderate as the river broadens again; but there is a huge rock on the right bank.

MILES 22.5, 19.8, AND 18.9   DNR campsites are available.

MILE 15.4   There is access at Brookston city park, complete with campsites, which is located three blocks south of the Route 31 bridge.

MILE 14.8   This is the confluence of the Cloquet River.

MILE 13.0   There is DNR access on the left bank at the Route 2 bridge.

MILE 5.3   A DNR campsite is found on the left bank.

MILE 4.5   A DNR rest area is located on the island.

MILE 0   Cloquet takeout, ramp, and campsites are found at Spafford Park. Canoeing below Cloquet is not practical because of the numerous dams and dangerous water conditions.

INFORMATION SOURCES

"Canoeing Trails," "Explorers Highroad," and "Camping in Minnesota," are available from 51 8th St., St. Paul, Minnesota 55101.

"Minnesota Voyageur Trails" is available from the Minnesota Department of Conservation, Division of Parks and Recreation, 320 Centennial Bldg., St. Paul, Minnesota 55101.

Minnesota Canoe Association, 101 79th Ave., North Minneapolis, Minnesota 55430, is a lively, strong organization dedicated to the promotion of canoeing in all its aspects: competition, wilderness tripping, and exchange of canoeing information among members. It unites persons interested in canoeing, the promotion of conservation of wilderness canoe areas, and the preservation of wild river systems.

Information on the canoeability of rivers can be obtained from the Division of Natural Resources. When in doubt, call: (612) 296-4776.

Information on the Boundary Waters Canoe Area is available from the forest supervisor, Superior National Forest, Duluth, Minnesota.

A series of four special reports on the Bigfork, Little Fork, St. Croix, and Minnesota rivers is available from Clyde Ryberg, 3232 Holmes St., Minneapolis, Minnesota.

"Camping in Minnesota" is available from Minnesota Camping, 51 E. 8th St., St. Paul, Minnesota 55101.

"Canoeing Trails" is available from Minnesota Camping, 51 E. 8th St., St. Paul, Minnesota 55101.

Ketter Canoeing, Inc., 101 79th Avenue, North Minneapolis, Minnesota, publishes the magazine *Canoeing*, which is filled with local tales and various "how to" articles. It also deals in canoe sales, canoe rentals, educational canoe trips for all ages, equipment, gear, and publications. As a bonus, you will get lots of canoeing conversation when you drop in on Betty Ketter, the Ralph Frese of Minnesota.

7
Adventure Trails of Wisconsin

The rolling, fertile prairie land of southern Wisconsin is noted for its productive crops and the country's most outstanding dairy farming industry. For the canoeist, however, the northern part of the state, high in elevation and forested, though much of it is cut over, gives rise to sparkling clear lakes, rushing rivers, and whitewater streams —all framed by bankside forests that combine to offer ideal canoe country.

The early French voyagers encountered the Indian tribes of the Winnebago, Ottowa, Potawatomi, and Menominee, then located in the northern forests and along the rivers. The Fox, Kickapoo, Mascoutin, Sauk, Illini, and Miami were spread throughout the central, south, and southwestern portions of the state.

The first white explorer to enter the state is believed to have been Jean Nicolet, who in 1634 landed on the shores of Green Bay. In 1654 Radisson and Groseilliers explored

Wisconsin and on a second trip (1658–60) built a log cabin on Chequamegon Bay (Ashland), the first white habitation in the state. By 1671 Jesuit priests were conducting twenty missions among as many Indian tribes. Meanwhile, the French explorers, notably Nicolas Perrot, Father Marquette, Joliet, and LaSalle, were active in the region. Duluth built a fort on Lake Pepin in 1680 for the protection of newcomers, most of them fur traders.

Wisconsin Canoe Trails

The water trails of Wisconsin, 3,361 miles of them, range from silent streams to roaring rapids. The riverbanks have changed: today they are lined with cottages, resorts, towns, dams, and bridges. But the rivers have not changed in the canoeing potential offered.

When the French came upon the scene, they christened the rivers Bois Brule, St. Croix, Manitowish, Peshtigo, and Flambeau. The rivers flow today as they did when they supported the birchbark and other craft of the explorers as they probed the unknown but spectacular land, moving frontiers farther and farther toward the sunset. For the canoeist wishing to identify with a valorous past, enjoy the beauty, and meet some challenges, here are a few Wisconsin canoe-camping adventures.

Flambeau River

The French explorers dubbed this river* the Flambeau ("flaming torch") in 1600 after witnessing the Indians fishing at night while holding aloft huge torches. This famed Midwest river—with its forks, numerous feeder streams, and a flowage created by a dam—has hundreds of miles of undeveloped shoreline, numerous islands, forests, abundant wildlife, and natural scenery. Such huge fish as the muskie,

---

*Information is available at the Flambeau State Forest Headquarters, Winter, Wisconsin.

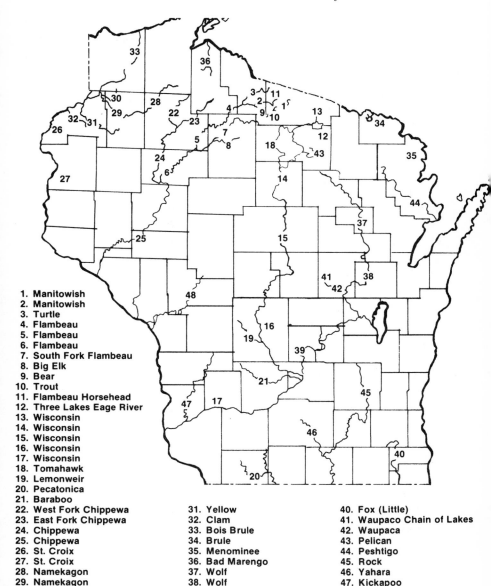

1. Manitowish
2. Manitowish
3. Turtle
4. Flambeau
5. Flambeau
6. Flambeau
7. South Fork Flambeau
8. Big Elk
9. Bear
10. Trout
11. Flambeau Horsehead
12. Three Lakes Eage River
13. Wisconsin
14. Wisconsin
15. Wisconsin
16. Wisconsin
17. Wisconsin
18. Tomahawk
19. Lemonweir
20. Pecatonica
21. Baraboo
22. West Fork Chippewa
23. East Fork Chippewa
24. Chippewa
25. Chippewa
26. St. Croix
27. St. Croix
28. Namekagon
29. Namekagon
30. Totogatic

31. Yellow
32. Clam
33. Bois Brule
34. Brule
35. Menominee
36. Bad Marengo
37. Wolf
38. Wolf
39. Fox

40. Fox (Little)
41. Waupaco Chain of Lakes
42. Waupaca
43. Pelican
44. Peshtigo
45. Rock
46. Yahara
47. Kickapoo
48. Black

Canoe trails of Wisconsin.

northern pike, and sturgeon are common to Flambeau waters, as are walleye, bass, and panfish.

A canoeist could spend an entire summer exploring the Flambeau River complex, but space limits the listing to a few highlights.

Park Falls to Nine Mile Creek is a twelve-mile run that takes about six hours. The put-in is south of Park Falls, where Route 13 crosses the river. The access is a road bank to the river. The cruising is mostly on flat water, due to the backup from the Pixley and Crowley dams. The flowage, with lots of dead trees, offers good fishing for the fighting game fish, for which Wisconsin is noted, if you can locate them.

The Pixley dam, dating back to 1916, is best portaged on the left bank. About six miles down is the Crowley dam, where the portage is on the right side. Downstream, the river flows through high banks at a medium speed, which makes for enjoyable canoeing. The takeout is at the landing on the left bank of Nine Mile Creek at Route 70.

Nine Mile Creek to Ladysmith is about forty-seven miles. However, many landings en route allow for shorter trips. Stops at Babb's Island, the Forks, and Big Falls dam break up the trip beautifully. The approach to Oxbo is a good stretch to try for northern pike and muskie in the moderate current. Below Oxbo the current speeds up, but it is not fast enough to be difficult.

The Babb's Island access at the public landing is on the left bank, just below the Route W bridge. Flambeau State Forest Headquarters are on the right bank, just below the bridge. This is the state agency that oversees the administration of this priceless native resource. Old-growth pine, hemlock, and hardwoods are preserved along the river course to retain the wilderness landscape. There is a large tract of virgin timber that is kept in its natural state so that modern canoeists can see the nature of the country as it existed over 100 years ago.

Porcupine Rapids represent the first really fast water on

this stretch of river. Keep to the smooth water of the main channel, whether in the center or to the left or right. The power of the current here and downstream is great; it moves fast and with authority. There have been a lot of aluminum scrapings left on boulders in the rapids of this stretch of the Flambeau.

There is a good campsite at the Camp 41 bridge and landing, below Porcupine Rapids. One-half mile downstream is the site of the Camp 41 logging operation, in use from 1930 to 1936, where the hardwood logs were hauled out by rail to Park Falls and Loretta.

The river widens and the current slows just before the turbulence of Wannigan Rapids. Stay with the main chute near the center and watch for submerged rocks. Immediately downstream are the Flambeau Falls, with a drop of 7 feet in 200 yards. Check the river situation before running it. A good portage trail is along the right bank, should you forgo shooting the turbulence.

The river moderates just above the juncture of the two Flambeaus ("the Forks"), where on the left there is a picturesque campsite under tall hemlocks on a high bank. There is no takeout here and most canoeists continue on to Big Falls. An alternative is Hervas Camp, which is two miles downstream on the left.

The next suggested segment of the Flambeau is from the Forks to the Big Falls dam, about thirteen miles. This stretch offers whitewater action, scenic shorelines, and good fishing. Leaving the campground at Hervas, named after four brothers, trappers and ginseng hunters who settled here during the Great Depression, Cedar Rapids is about a mile away. For the seasoned canoeist who decides to run Cedar Rapids (named after a grove of cedar that once grew along the banks), the first pitch is the trickiest. Take the channel to the left of the island, about midway between the island and the left bank. Hit the pitch with the flow of the main current and watch for the submerged rocks in the channel. For the photographer, Cedar Rapids offers a good vantage point. A clean campground is located on the right bank, and the high bluff on the left bank provides a scenic background.

Whether in Michigan, Minnesota, or Wisconsin, the base of falls should be probed with deep-running lures for walleye and northern pike.
(Michigan Tourist Council)

The turbulent rapids continue at Camp 4. Then there is a third and a fourth pitch before reaching Beaver Dam Rapids, which, with its four-foot drop, is extremely dangerous during high water. About three miles downstream is the Flambeau Lodge, a popular takeout point. Permission to take out can be obtained from the proprietor. At the Big Falls dam the portage is over the dike near the left bank. Below the dike is an excellent free campsite maintained by the Lake Superior District Power Company.

For the stretch from the power company access to Ladysmith, the backed-up waters of man-made Lake Flambeau provide flatwater cruising. It is an interesting change of pace from the fast water and rapids.

Granite Bay on the left is appropriately named, as the steep outcrop juts up from the water. This local source of granite was used in the construction of the earth-filled Flambeau flowage dam.

The Tony bridge, leading to the town of the same name, spans the flowage. After an S-curve to Mandowish Point, the lake opens up to its full width; but occasional strong winds can make the crossing difficult. Favor the shore as a windbreak, if possible.

There are public landings at either end of the Dairyland Dam, at the Flambeau hydroelectric station; camping and picnic facilities are on the south end. After the takeout, the portage path is from the landing at the north end of the lake, down one-fourth mile of good road. The put-in is below the powerhouse. Once underway, you can fish the tailwaters for walleye. The quick water over rock at the base of falls and rapids and the tailwaters of dams are likely places to probe for walleye and bass. Many times you will be able to capture your dinner.

Typical fast river water is found for a while. Then the river slows because of the Ladysmith dam. You are back to civilization on this homestretch; cabins, roads, and people are evident along the banks. At Ladysmith, Memorial Park is the usual takeout point; campsites, water, and supplies are available.

St. Croix River

The St. Croix River* is one of America's wild rivers, and measures have been taken to preserve portions of it in their natural state for posterity. The U.S. Senate passed S.897 in September 1965 to establish a St. Croix National Scenic Riverway in Wisconsin and Minnesota. This makes provisions for the northern portion of the St. Croix and the Namekagon tributary to be maintained as a "wild river" in its primitive condition, while the southern portion is to be used for more intensive types of recreation. The clear

*Information is available from the superintendent, St. Croix National Scenic Riverway, Box 579, St. Croix Falls, Wisconsin 54024.

water runs deep and fast through uninhabitable areas and at times between towering banks. Along its course from Solon Springs are stretches of noisy whitewater and relatively harmless rapids. The river quiets for a distance and then roars again; these conditions alternate to provide a stimulating change of pace.

The St. Croix is born at Solon Springs at Route 53; you can put in there, but the profuse vegetation and slow and shallow water make an alternate put-in preferable. The town of Gordon at Route 53 or seven miles west at Route Y is recommended. Wherever you put in, by all means see the hillside with its numerous trickles that collect into rivulets and go singing downhill. The springs are of geographical interest, being located on a hill. The north side springs combine to form the Bois Brule River, which flows northward to Lake Superior. The south side springs combine to form the St. Croix, which flows southward, eventually to the Gulf of Mexico. Thus the navigable two-mile stretch served as a famous portage to link Lake Superior and the Mississippi River. The portage was used by Indians, voyagers, explorers, missionaries, and fur traders. Sieur du Lhut (Duluth) in 1680 was the first white man known to use the portage; today, history buffs are probably the most enthusiastic users of the two-mile portage.

The dam at the end of Gordon flowage is portaged on the left, as are the next two portages. Downstream to Danbury there are several stretches of rapids, of which the Fishtrap is probably the most exciting, being rocky, shallow, and sporty. This stretch of the St. Croix from the Gordon dam portage put-in is free-flowing, wild, and clean for eighty-five miles, at the end of which it is impounded by Nevers dam. The scenic river valley offers a fitting backdrop to the fast-flowing whitewater river with its thirty-five rapids. The mark of humans is seldom seen, and this is the stretch that will be permanently maintained in its wild condition.

Along the spectacular miles of the St. Croix's course, access points and campsites are spread adequately apart, the fishing is excellent, and the stimulation of the passing land-scape continues to be superb. The current moderates a bit in long, smooth tongues of water. Then the turbulence of State Line Rapids appear where the St. Croix River is shared with Minnesota as a mutual state boundary. The remainder of the river's course to the Mississippi River is discussed in the Minnesota chapter (see pages 113–120).

Brule River

Early in the country's history the Brule* served as a water trail from the gateway at Lake Superior to the upper Mid-west. It was a strategic route for travelers intent on prob-ing Wisconsin's interior and the miles beyond. To this day the Brule remains a wild river, threading its way through trees, shallows, rapids, and bogs. During the low-water stages, when snags and boulders are exposed, canoeists need to call upon their poling technique to negotiate the ruffled water.

From its origin at Solon Mills to Stones Bridge, nine miles down, the upper Brule presents the typical characteristics of a newly formed river, including a slow, narrow, winding course, overhanging limbs, beaver dams, and submerged logs. This stretch is canoed chiefly by naturalists interested in the bog swamps, and there are no campsites on the soft shoreline. The difficulty of this portion of the Brule can be gauged by the travel time: the nine-mile distance requires about ten hours to complete.

The preferred put-in is at Stones bridge where County Route S crosses the river. The distance to Route 2 is twelve miles, requiring about seven hours of paddling. After leav-ing the bridge, the canoeist encounters several miles of gentle water that runs through banks lined with towering spruce. All this reminds the canoeist that this pristine waterway and its banks are in the Brule River State

---

*Information is available from the superintendent, St. Croix National Scenic Riverway, Box 579, St. Croix Falls, Wisconsin 54024.

Forest. There are many private holdings, but private and public owners alike preserve the natural beauty of the area, and common courtesy requires that the rights of private owners be respected by the canoeists passing through.

Campsites within the park are free to persons traveling the Brule by watercraft. There are some primitive camp-sites, which are marked by rustic, teepee-shaped emblems.

Numerous small streams from boggy and weedy land filter the water to give purity and clearness to the Brule. The contributing springs add volume as the river widens into several bays where the canoeist can pull in to cool off and rest in the shade.

Large Norway and eastern white pine signal the Cedar Island Estate with its buildings and rustic footbridge. The main lodge and grounds of the estate are on the left shore, above Green Bridge. So popular is the Brule for trout fishing that President Calvin Coolidge spent the summer of 1928 on Cedar Island. Presidents Hoover and Eisenhower, too, were guests at the lodge during their terms in office. To this day, the Brule attracts and pleases expert fly fishers, as well as notables.

Below Cedar Island is one-half mile of fast water, leading to a pool with a picnic site. Immediately below the pool lies Lower Twin Rapids, the first good rapids, which should be checked before running. The river then rushes into Big Lake, a widening of the river to about one-fourth of a mile wide and one mile long. During the quiet hours of morning and evening deer can be seen standing in the shallows.

Cottages dot the shore for a distance, but then the river takes on its wilderness aspect again as Norway and white pines replace man-made structures on its banks. Past the bridge at County Route 13, Williamson and Running Hall's rapids can provide a real challenge; they are fast and challenge the paddle of even the seasoned canoeist. The river rushes directly toward a concrete wall, then veers sharply away. The next whitewater, Little Joe Rapids, is tricky. Check it out before you take to the swift water and the passage between the rocks that lie close to the narrow right bank.

Downstream, beyond Rainbow Bend and Doodlebug Rapids, the usual takeout is at the public landing and parking area on the left bank just above the Route 2 bridge at Brule. Should an overnight stay be in the plans, the Brule State Forest Campground is on the right shore, near Rainbow Bend; facilities include a landing, campsite, fresh water, and toilets.

The veteran canoeist who wishes to challenge the Brule all the way to Lake Superior will discover that the stretch from Route 2 to Copper Range Campground has good trout and passable canoeing water. However, the character of the river downstream is menacing.

From the Copper Range Campground to the Route 13 bridge are the most dangerous rapids on the entire river. No party should attempt this stretch without a guide who is familiar with the river. Upsets and dunkings are the rule, not the exception. The river tumbles down a geological formation called Copper Range, dropping 110 feet in three miles! In addition, there are portages through rough terrain, one of which is over a mile long. The canoeist is alerted to upcoming portages by the roar of turbulent water. This stretch of boulder- and ledge-strewn water, with its difficult curves, is not often disturbed; therefore, the huge brown and rainbow trout have a secure haven in which to thrive and grow to lunker size. Near the end of the river's course there is a fisher's parking area and access. A hike in is necessary from the route, called simply "Road to Mouth of Brule."

For those wishing to take the five-hour trip to Lake Superior, the put-in is at the Route 13 wayside, just above the bridge. There is some exciting water before McNeils bridge and landing, which is not a recommended access due to the rugged road.

Riffles and easy rapids characterize the stretch. The deep

holes are havens for brown trout, even though the water takes on a reddish-brown hue as it nears Lake Superior. The next portage is around the electric lamprey weir when it is in operation. Signs are placed on the approach to the weir to indicate whether or not to portage. The electric weirs, which kill small lamprey before they migrate into the Great Lakes, are effective devices and they are placed in feeder streams all around Lake Superior. The program is jointly administered by the U.S. and Canada.

Less than a mile below the weir Lake Superior comes into view. Takeout is at the boat landing and parking area.

Namekagon River

The Namekagon* runs for about 110 miles from its head-waters at Namekagon Lake (3,285 acres) to the St. Croix River. As much of the upper course is near highways and built-up areas and is subject to low water periods, the Hayward access is used by many canoe parties.

For those who forgo the Hayward dam access, the pre-ferred put-in point is at the wayside picnic ground and campsite at the Hayward Ranger Station at Route 27. Im-mediately downstream, the Warder Rapids offer a series of large boulders, some of which are submerged; but there is room to maneuver the canoe through. The Fox Slough eddies and mild rapids offer no problem, and below is a historic site—the Namekagon Court O'Reilles Portages. This two and one-half mile portage trail, leads to Windigo Lake and the extensive Chippewa River system, joining the Namekagon River and thus providing a vital transpor-tation link for the Indians and early explorers. On the left bank is the site where Michael Cadotte in 1784 established the first trading post in the region.

The river slows a bit as you pass Hurley Creek. There is a possible rest stop on the right at River Rat Campgrounds,

---

*Information is available from the superintendent, St. Croix National Scenic Riverway, Box 579, St. Croix Falls, Wisconsin 54024.

which are privately owned but available for public use. The river drops at the Old Sinnet Bridge rapids at Route E, providing a bit of action before a possible takeout on the left bank at scenic Groat Landing. The landing is privately owned and offers a small picnic area.

From Groat Landing to Trego* is about seventeen miles, and paddling time is about seven hours. The put-in is at Groat Landing. Should you begin your trip at this point, the landing is on the south bank of the river.

Secure all gear for the first fast water at the Chippanazie Rapids, which can best be run down the main dark water chutes. After navigating left around a large island just above Tripp Creek and turning right with the bend, you will come to a wayside park with water and toilets. At the iron bridge there is an optional access point. Supplies are available at Springbrook on Highway 63, a short distance south.

Even though the river continues not far from highways, the mild rapids and deep-cut banks insure seclusion and continuing interest in the cruise. Bean Brook joins the Namekagon and, as it is reputed to be an excellent trout stream, spending some time on a side trip here could mean trout for dinner. One possibility is to put in at Route 63 and drift down the Bean to the Namekagon, quietly casting ahead.

Below Earl there is a park and campground with water and toilet facilities. On the approach to Trego there is a historical marker on the left bank, indicating a much-used Indian campground—a stopping place of fur traders, explorers, and missionaries. Jonathon Carver camped here in 1767, as did Henry Schoolcraft in 1831.

Beyond the railroad bridge the Trego flowage water slows progress to the takeout on the right bank at Trego Park, where there are complete facilities.

The next segment downstream is from Trego to Byrkit Landing, fifteen miles away, and requires about five hours. If you can canoe only one stretch of the Namekagon River,

---

*The National Park Service, under the Wild and Scenic Rivers Act, manages the entire river.

The foundation construction of trestles and bridges requires much excavation; consequently canoeists must be careful of hidden obstructions when passing under them.

by all means this should be it, because here you will see a fully protected wild and scenic river.

A put-in at Trego Lake (385 acres) would require five miles of paddling past summer homes and resorts to the dam and portage. Below Trego Dam, at the Route K bridge on the left, or west, bank is a good put-in point complete with campsite. This access cuts down considerably the paddling route to Byrkit Landing, allowing more time to enjoy the scenery en route.

You are now on an undefaced, free-flowing stretch of water, free of crossroads, campsites, facilities, dams, and buildings. All the way to its junction with the St. Croix River, this lower Namekagon is fully protected and preserved under the Wild River Act of 1968. The pristine, high-wooded banks and the clean water support many species of wildlife, waterfowl, and aquatic life in ecological balance. The river continues swiftly to the takeout at Byrkit Landing, noted on some maps as Whispering Pines Landing.

The put-in point for the next leg of the trip is Byrkit Landing. The wilderness continues; the heavily forested country and the river, racing between steep banks, bestow a feeling of solitude akin to that enjoyed by the Indians and voyagers who once traveled here.

Ahead lie Casey Creek's entry at Deer Ford (so named

because the deer use it as a favored drinking place) and Wilderness Point Boys Camp, and the pilings of Howell Bridge, left from early logging days. On the right bank there is a campsite with water and toilet facilities; a small fee is charged for overnight camping.

Downstream, the river moves at a moderate speed with occasional ruffled water. Where the river cuts the high banks to form deep chutes is where the walleye lie. This is a good place to fish for them, as the takeout is a short distance away. Beyond where the Totogatic River enters from the right, the Namekagon Trail Bridge takeout comes into view. Most parties leave the river here, as there is no takeout at the junction with the St. Croix.

Wolf River

The Wolf River* flows through the Menominee Indian Reservation (Menominee County), and here the canoeist will experience some of Wisconsin's most inspiring scenery: valuable timber stands, a grove of virgin trees, rock-strewn fast water that whitens the river, and chutes of water between rocky cliffs. Conditions are ideal for trout, for which the Wolf is famous.

The put-in is at Post lake, Route K, or Pearson, Route A. It is a fairly calm run to Langlade Route 55, as the river does not churn and froth quite as furiously as it does below Langlade. This is a good stretch for newcomers to get the feel of whitewater.

From Langlade to Route M, a fourteen-mile stretch presents one of the finest pieces of fast water to be found in the Midwest. Whitewater enthusiasts can here challenge a one and one-fourth mile chute of continuous rapids where the water drops thirty-two feet per mile, a test for the most skillful canoeist.

---

*Information is available from the Department of Natural Resources, Box 450, Madison, Wisconsin 53703, or American Youth Hostels, 2210 N. Clark St., Chicago, Illinois 60634.

It is possible to make the fourteen-mile run in about six hours. However, many make a day of it by going over a difficult stretch several times to practice technique. There are picnic facilities and campgrounds to offer a respite from the water.

On the river's course through the Menominee Reservation, there are several Class 4 rapids, which race down narrow rock walls and end in falls of up to ten feet. Below the turbulence, the river moderates, and it is possible to cruise in peace to Keshena and from there through pastoral landscapes all the way to Shawano.

Wisconsin River

The dams on the Wisconsin River make it the most harnessed river in the state. It is truly an eighty-one mile commercial artery; its banks know many cities with high populations, varied industries, and numerous commercial enterprises. For a quick overview, here is a sketchy description of the Wisconsin's eighty-one mile run, not all of which is industralized.

"Last one to the campsite pitches the tent and washes dishes!"

LAC VIEUX DESERT TO VILAS-ONEIDA COUNTY LINE
The river is shallow with a few riffles at the outset, and then it picks up volume. There are two short portages and no dan-

gerous rapids. After leaving Conover and Watersmeet, there is the Eagle River dam, which requires a 100-foot portage.

VILAS-ONEIDA COUNTY LINE TO MERRIL   The dam at Rainbow Lake requires a portage. Then the river slows at the Rhinelander flowage. Below is Tomahawk, and the river is dammed four times before reaching Merril. A highway follows the river along this entire stretch.

MERRIL TO NEKOOSA   This stretch of the Wisconsin is the most exploited, passing through Brokaw, Wausau, Mosinee, Stevens Point, Wisconsin Rapids, and Port Edwards—all known for their dams and large paper mills. Obstructions in the river between Brokaw and Rothschild have been marked by the Wausau Boat Club.

NEKOOSA TO PRAIRIE DU SAC   This stretch abounds in such scenic attractions as Petenwell Lake, Castle Rock, Lake Wisconsin, and the famed Upper and Lower Wisconsin Dells. Including both natural and man-made attractions, the Dells are highly commercialized. At the Wisconsin Dells the river is very deep and swift, hemmed in by forty- to fifty-foot rock banks. Sightseeing launches and speedboats fill the scenic Dells, and their turbulence can be a hazard to canoes.

PRAIRIE DU SAC TO MISSISSIPPI RIVER   The put-in below the dam at Prairie du Sac dam represents the most popular canoeing segment of the Wisconsin River. Many groups take to the river for this easy and enjoyable cruise. There are no portages or difficult water, but there are long, linear sandbars at all water levels. The banks are overhung with tall, cool trees. The river runs parallel to highways, and it is possible to use wayside tables and fireplaces for lunch stops. There are ample campsites on the banks, islands, and sandbars. Tower Hill State Park has an excellent campground.

up to Route 60 is the Wauzeka public landing, with primitive campsites and canoe rentals nearby. Supplies are available at any of the towns on or near the river. Takeout can be on the Mississippi River upstream at Prairie du Chien. This is the second-oldest city in Wisconsin, and its name reminds us that it has lived under the French, British and American flags. Wyalsing State Park, down the Mississippi backwaters, is much more appropriate for canoeists. Here you can observe, as did Pere Marquette and Jolliet, the joining of the Wisconsin and Mississippi rivers.

On the river approach to Wyalusing State Park there are many islands, but this will not be confusing if you keep to the left shore. Before the confluence of the Wisconsin and Mississippi rivers is the central campground. The park has complete facilities for the entire family: picnic areas, nature and Indian trails, bluff overlooks, baseball diamonds, tennis courts, Indian mounds, and a wildlife refuge. There are three well-defined canoe trails weaving among the many islands. The sheltered water offers an ideal opportunity for the novice to practice boarding, paddling strokes, and general canoe skills.

The 1,671-acre park could very well serve as headquarters for visitors to this area, so rich is it in canoe-oriented history. Prairie du Chien, via highway 18, is but twelve miles north. When Jonathon Carver visited the Indian village in 1766 and noted a large pack of barking dogs, he called it "Dog Plain." However, the residents preferred the French "Prairie du Chien." Legend and history are clearly evident in points of interest such as the Villa Louis Mansion (1840), the American Fur Company Warehouse (1828), St. Gabriel's (the state's oldest Catholic church), the tomb of Fr. Galtier, founder of St. Paul, and so on.

Chippewa River

The Chippewa River canoe trail from Ojibwa to Imalone

has twenty-five rapids within eleven miles and is a sporty course—fast and wild. Yet, as it does not carry a high hazard rating, it is a good introduction to whitewater canoeing. Old dam sites and rusted remains of pikes and peaveys along the banks of the stream testify to its lumbering past.

In early days craft other than the birchbark canoe plied the waters of Wisconsin. In 1870 the bateau, a flat-bottomed riverboat thirty feet long and thirty inches wide, was introduced by J. W. Harmon. For a short period of time the bateau increased in popularity on the Chippewa because of its suitability for cargo freighting.

Although there are forty-seven miles of the Chippewa River canoe trail in addition to the stretch from Winter Dam to Ojibwa, the eight-mile, three-hour trip is popular and so is included here. Its advantages include fishing for muskie and pike, scenic shorelines, and easy access.

Put-in is at the public landing on the right, just below Winter dam. Routes L and G parallel the river. The prolific fishing waters begin immediately; beyond where Knapp–Stout Creek enters the river is Lombard's Hole, a deep pool that is a favorite of local fishers.

Just above Bishop's Bridge, where Route G crosses the river, is Wannigan's Landing, the site of a loggers' supply shop in the late 1880s. Take the left channel at the island below the bridge, where the current is deep and strong. The rapids below Phalen Creek are easily run, and one mile more will take you to the scenic Ojibwa State Park, where complete facilities are available. A small fee is charged for overnight camping.

The trip terminates at the village of Ojibwa, on the left bank where Route G spans the river. The public landing for takeout is on the right bank just below the bridge. Al Raynor's Stopping Place is there. In the 1890s the rivermen and tote-team drivers on this Chippewa trail used Raynor's as a rest stop, so to speak. The building still stands on the right bank, just above the bridge.

At the other end of the Chippewa River system is another short (10.5-mile) stretch, which can be paddled in less than eight hours. The history of the area is interesting, and usually the fishing for muskie, walleye, and bass is too. There is little difficulty along the entire route, except for wind occasionally blowing across the open water of Holcombe Flowage at the end of the trip.

To get there, take U.S. Route 8 near the town of Bruce to local Route E. Take Route E southward along the Flambeau River to where it meets the Chippewa (called "the Forks"). The Clam Shell landing there is the popular put-in point. Immediately, the historic aspects of the trip unfold.

Visit the site of Shaw Farm on the right bank, which in 1860 provided oxen, horses, cattle, wheat, and vegetables for the logging camps. Farther along, the French influence is evident at Flambeau village, established in 1850. Plats of the area carry the names of settlers like Gourdoux, Courriere, and Bouchier.

On the right bank, one-half mile below the steel bridge, stands the Old Indian Mission Church, the oldest in Rusk County (1881) and still in use. A mile farther downstream on the left bank is the old Cote Homestead. The buildings are made of local logs and stone, exemplifying the early construction methods that utilized the materials of the region.

It is always interesting to probe feeder streams. To take one example, Deertail Creek has muskie, blue, and catfish holes.

The main river channel soon turns and widens to show the evidences of the water backup. The current stops, and the large expanse of the Holcombe flowage invites fishing—before or after making camp.

Campsites are numerous; there is the Sportsmen Club Park and Campground on the left bank, Birch Creek Park on the west side, Chippewa County Park on the south side, and Holcombe Park on the lower east side of the lake. The takeout is on the right bank just below the Route M bridge, just above the Northern States Power Company dam.

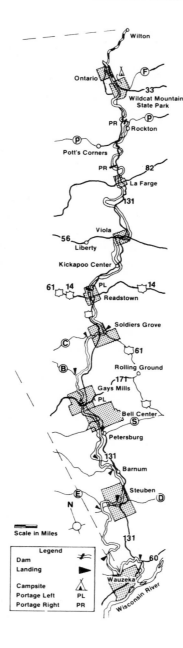

Kickapoo River.

Kickapoo River and Environs

The Kickapoo,* like many midwestern waterways, is more than a river; it also represents a geographic treasure and a historic valley. It runs through that part of southwestern Wisconsin that boasts such names as "Little Switzerland," "Blackhawk Country," "Frank Lloyd Wright's native city," and "the Kickapoo Valley."

Should you wish an interesting prelude to your canoe trip down the Kickapoo, drive the thirteen miles from Ontario to La Farge via Route 131. You will absorb views of unspoiled, verdant, rolling countryside and diverse topography with growing forms and rocky landscape, all embroidered by the lush growth of the river bottom—a photographer's dream.

Farther downstream, a favorite view is the one from the apple orchard roads above Gays Mills, where in springtime you will see over 65,000 apple trees and over 8,000 cherry trees in bloom, brightening and perfuming the hillsides.

Accesses are numerous, canoe rentals are ample, and there are shuttle and pickup services all along the route. The uppermost put-in is Route 33 at Ontario, above the bridge on the left bank. Downstream accesses, listed according to river mileage from Ontario, include (six miles) Wildcat Mt. State Park (with picnic area); (13 miles) left bank Rockton, Route P bridge east bank (supplies, parking, campsite available, dam portage); (15 miles) Bridge 13, Indian Head (access above bridge left bank); (19 miles) Bridge 18, Bacon (access right bank, parking area, camp in village park); (22 miles) La Farge Power Plant, dam (portage left bank).

---

*Information resources include Mrs. Jerry Schoville, Kickapoo Valley Association, Box 8, Soldiers Grove, Wisconsin 54655; and Bernard Smith, Route 2, Box 211, La Farge, Wisconsin 54639. Bernard and Jeanne Smith, Route 2, Box 211, La Farge, Wisconsin 54639, are local residents with on-the-spot awareness of the daily condition of the Kickapoo River and other rivers in the area. Their services include placement and pickup scheduling maps, tour information for couples or groups, and related concerns. Erm and Patricia Kramer, 2820 Riverwoods Road, Deerfield, Illinois 60015, are knowledgeable canoeists and Kickapoo Valley landowners.

At Smith's Landing (three miles) Bernard and Jeanne Smith have for a decade been renting canoes for trips from two hours to eight days for one party or for large groups. For those beginning their trip here, the Smiths will describe the river's snaky, meandering course. There are more than seventy miles of river; yet, as the crow flies, it is only thirty-three miles. So crooked is the river's course that in some single miles of its course you will go in all four directions of the compass.

Floating downstream on a rambling and spunky current that is rarely foamed by rapids, the sternman will use his paddle as a rudder to bear off the high bluff banks. Then on straightaways there are low-hanging tree branches to duck under and occasional log or brush jams that must be pushed aside or the canoe pulled over or carried around.

Above Viola (38 miles), bridge 27 access is on the right bank; supplies are available in town. Readstown (58 miles) bridge 32 access is on the left bank; the bridge known as Manning Bridge is just north of town and is noted for its annual fathers' sponsored canoe race down a course of challenging water ending at Soldiers Grove Village Park. The access at Soldiers Grove (63 miles) is at the village park, below bridge 36 on the right bank. At Gays Mills (74 miles) there is a dam requiring a portage on the left side above bridge 38. At Steuben (91 miles) above bridge 43, a concentrated area of wilderness begins on the left bank. This area is without crossroads, source of supplies, or drinking water.

Plum Creek landing (102 miles) is on the right bank, and the takeout point is Wauzeka (112 miles) on the right bank. Wauzeka adds to the history of the area; the past seems to come alive as you silently drift with the current, viewing or imagining half-forgotten farmsteads, old mill sites, alleged whiskey stills, and gold coins buried under the river sandbars. In the tranquil silence you can imagine the lumberjacks rafting their logs downriver to Diamond Joe's shipbuilding yards in Wauzeka.

If you have traveled the length of the Kickapoo River,

you have experienced a river and valley rich in waterfowl, song birds, trout and bass, deciduous hardwoods and conifers, and animals such as deer, mink, raccoon, and fox; and you have been in a land wild enough to support beaver. And over the entire landscape there are the faint traces of moccasined feet.

The mystique of the Kickapoo River comes from distinctive influences: the nearby historic Wisconsin and Mississippi rivers which it feeds; nearby Taliesin East near Spring Green, the home and school built by the world-renowned architect Frank Lloyd Wright; Wright's Warehouse Museum, a classic early work in his native city, Richland Center; and the Mineral Point area, where in the early 1900s 7,000 Cornish miners from Wales came to work in the lead mines. Wisconsin's nickname, "The Badger State," came from the Cornish miners' habit of making their homes in the sides of hills like badgers during the cold, snowy winter season. There is also an 1890 reconstructed farm village and hotel at Cassville; an 1827 lead mine and an 1837 stone cottage at Potosi; the Cunningham Museum at Platteville; and at Stonefield, a village of the 1890s complete with general store, livery stable, blacksmith shop, and historic riverfront hotel, is Old Denniston House (circa 1836). This brief list seems to indicate that even long ago the Kickapoo River valley was popular, as well as populated.

Trout River

This canoe trail is popular with the boys' camps in the area. Along the Trout River, which passes through Alder and Wild Rice lakes, there is good fishing for muskie, pike, and bass. In the fall the Indians harvest wild rice by bending the tall stems over the gunwale of the canoe and beating the grain with a stick into the bottom of the canoe. A tarp or plastic sheet is spread over the floor to catch the rice. After winnowing, drying, and parching, the delectable wild rice is ready for cooking. Considering the extensive labor involved in harvesting and preparing wild rice, one can understand why it is so expensive in the marketplace.

The put-in is on Route 51 where the river leaves Trout Lake. The riverbanks are not banks at all, but rather expanses of rice fields through which the river meanders. After passing the small lakes of wild rice and alder, Manitowish Lake is reached. From here there are many directions to go—to Manitowish River or to Stone Island, or Clear Lake. Campsites are plentiful, but many of them are private.

As most of these lakes are heavily fished with powerboats for muskie, pike, and bass, the canoeist is advised to proceed northward along connecting channels to Presque Isle and Crab Lakes and take out there. Those intent on fishing may elect to backtrack and take out at the put-in point.

Black River

The Black River is of historic import in that it served as a contributing waterway in the early exploration of the Mississippi River Valley. Its 107-mile, fast-moving course begins in northern Taylor County and flows southwesterly to the Mississippi at Onalaska.

The upper part (51 miles), from Route 73 to the Black River Falls, is characterized by a rocky bottom with numerous high-hazard rapids. The water level is not consistently adequate for desirable canoeing. For the weekend and beginning canoeist intent on a summer trip, this stretch of the river should be forgone in favor of the lower portion.

Paddling the lower river (56 miles) is an easy three-day trip, but shorter trips are possible, as campsites and accesses are plentiful. The put-in is on the east bank below the Black River Falls dam, and once underway there is pleasant cruising with no dams or rapids. Campsites are strategically situated at Hoffman Wayside Park, west of North Bend, and on Route 93. Hawk Island, located a few miles below Black River Falls, has a campground. *Do not camp* on the sandbars, as the release of water from the dam can flood the sites. Route 54 runs near the river's course and touches the river at Irving and North Bend.

The Black River has a dark coloration due to organic material in its watershed. The river's wooded and wild banks and scenery and farmland vistas offer a low-key adventure. Takeouts include Amsterdam at Route XX; the Mississippi River, which involves paddling across the stump-filled Onalaska flowage; or along the northeast shore, Route 2.

Information Sources

Wisconsin probably has more canoe guides published about its river heritage and recreational potential than any other midwestern state.

"Wisconsin Water Trails" was published by the Conservation Department, Box 450, Madison, Wisconsin 53701. However, it is currently out of print and there are no plans at this time (1978) to reprint it.

"Wisconsin North Central Canoe Trails" is available from the Rusk City Information Center, Ladysmith, Wisconsin 54848.

"Whitewater; Quietwater" is available from the American Canoe Association, 4260 E. Evans Ave., Denver, Colorado 80222.

The following three regional guides are available from Outdoor Books, Wisconsin Tales and Trails, Box 5650, Madison, Wisconsin 53705.

"Canoe Trails of Northeastern Wisconsin"

"Canoe Trails of Southern Wisconsin"

"Canoeing the Wild Rivers of Northwestern Wisconsin"

"A Canoeing Guide to the Indian Head Rivers of West Central Wisconsin" is available from W. A. Fisher Co., Box 1107, Virginia, Minnesota 55792.

"Canoeing Guide to Indian Head Rivers" is available from Wisconsin Indian Head, Inc., 3015 E. Clairmont St., Eau Claire, Wisconsin 54701.

Topographic maps are available from the Wisconsin Geological and Natural History Survey, 1815 University Ave., Madison, Wisconsin 53706.

"Wisconsin Campground Directory" is available from the Wisconsin Conservation Department, Box 450, Madison, Wisconsin 53701.

General tourism information other than that contained here is available from the Wisconsin Division of Tourism, P.O. Box 7606, Madison, Wisconsin 53707.

8

Adventure Trails of Ontario

Adjoining northern Minnesota, southwestern Ontario is an integral part of the midwestern canoeland. The province, with its districts of Kenora and Rainy River, is a geographical and geological entity. Also, Ontario is separated from the upper peninsula of Michigan only by a narrow ship channel, the "Soo," with both U.S. and Canadian cities named Sault Ste. Marie on their respective sides. As with Minnesota, the unfenced, unguarded gateways lead to a wildness that comes from a low-density population.

Ontario comprises a part of the Laurentian Shield, an extensive area characterized by smooth, sloping rock, conifer forests, sparkling lakes, and clean rivers that rush and tumble in steep courses down rapids and falls. The area contains a complex of waters that represents a very large portion of the earth's fresh water. The natural features of Ontario offer spectacular canoeing adventures on hundreds of remote wilderness trails, and the province also offers an opportunity for statesiders to enjoy their neighbor's hospitality—on or off the water.

Canoe Trails of Ontario

Ontario has been endowed with a vast network of 250,000 lakes and connecting waterways that permit extensive canoe travel in almost any direction. The canoe routes are maintained by the Ontario Department of Lands and Forests and provide a choice of travel through a wide range of water and geological conditions. Many of the canoe routes lead through wilderness expanses far from civilization and provide opportunities found few other places in the settled parts of North America.

*Quetico Provincial Park**

If you have experienced the BWCA from stateside points of entry (see pages 99–102), perhaps an entry from the Canadian side would be of interest.

Quetico is synonymous with canoeing, which dates back to its early inhabitants, as evidenced by the Indian pictographs, fingerpainted symbols of iron oxide adorning rock faces, rare discoveries of arrowheads and copper work, and other early art found there. The rock hound, too, can have a field day here in the Pre-Cambrian Shield with the aid of a geological map. But these waterways mainly serve those who seek an interlude of peace in a world apart and those fishers who seek virgin waters. The vast wilderness of 1,750 square miles enables the canoe-camper to spend a weekend or a month in the land of the voyageurs. In the summer the area is accessible only by canoe and pack (bush planes are not allowed).

---

*Available from the district forester, Fort Francis, 922 Scott St., Fort Francis, Ontario, Canada, is a booklet entitled "Canoe Routes—Quetico Provincial Park" and Map No. 56A, "Quetico Provincial Park."

A typical Canadian canoe camp.

This area of concentrated lakes and rivers, towering granite cliffs, and rocky islands and reefs is one of the prime canoeing regions in Canada. Every bend in the river reveals the rich human and natural history of the land.

Twelve major canoe routes, including the voyageur route of the fur-trade era, are well defined. There are many less-traveled routes that provide side trips for the more experienced canoeist. There is a deep wilderness solitude in the Quetico—it is unspoiled, litter-free, and without cabins, resorts, docks, marinas, or other evidence of civilization. It remains as it was in the day of the explorers, and through reading their diaries the modern canoeist and history buff can reenact their travels and identify with their experiences.

Car access to the north side of the park is via Route 11 to the Dawson Trail Campground on French Lake. Canoeists entering from the U.S. through the BWCA must clear Canadian Customs at one of the four outpost stations along the international boundary. At the sites there are small stores where you can stock up on staples, apparel, and equipment, if needed.

Algoma District of Ontario

This canoeing hinterland, comprising over 16,000 square miles and lying along the north shore of Lake Superior and Lake Huron, is roadless. However, it is made available to the canoeist by the Algoma Central Railway (ACR),* one of Canada's most interesting railroads. The ACR has been running since the days when lumberjacks, trappers, and miners outnumbered fishers and canoeists. In its 289-mile run through wilderness after the station at Wabos, the present-day diesel engine climbs, curves, and dips as it puffs up small mountains, across high trestles, among spruce swamps, and through pine plains dotted with lakes. Photography buffs will be especially interested in Agawa Canyon, a rocky defile that comes alive with cascading water and the whitewater of rivers splashing on the canyon floor. The scenery is of rugged beauty as the Montreal River plunges and races toward Lake Superior. Bridal Falls and several others plunge into the canyon below in lacy sheets of white. Many canoeists plan their trip according to where their favorite species of fish can be found. The first part of the route is to Hawk Junction, which is tout water, while the route from Hawk Junction to Hearst, the end of the line, is known for its walleye fishing. Northern pike fishing is good all along the route in the large lakes. The train drops canoeists off along the way for trips of a few days to weeks. When you are finished with your trip— no prearrangement necessary—you simply carry the canoe and gear to the railroad siding, stack them, and wait for the daily run to come along. You will learn the timetable from the personnel when you purchase your ticket.

---

*Further information is available from the traffic manager, Algoma Central Railway, Sault Ste. Marie, Ontario, Canada.

The train leaves Sault Ste. Marie early in the morning, daily except Sundays, and your car is safe in the railroad parking lot until you return. The railroad employees will load your baggage before departure, and you will be underway before long on your way to your chosen destination. The canoe and equipment are unloaded, the canoe carried to the water's edge, the food and gear stowed, and you are ready to consider beaver lodges, otter slides, abandoned gold mines, and trout fishing on the way down to civilization.

Several Algoma rivers weave to and from the railroad, and a variety of trips are available. One, neither rough nor hazardous, is the Hilda to Michipicoten trip, which runs through plenty of wild country without many portages or much whitewater.

Canadian guides such as Bob Ahlin, assure a safe and satisfying experience in the hinterland.
(Canadian Government Office of Tourism)

Briefly, other trips include one on the Batchawana River from mile 80 to Lake Superior. This is a rather rough but scenic, trip. Another trip, from Sand River from mile 138 to Lake Superior, offers excellent trout fishing along the rough route that requires twenty-eight portages and takes about seven days.

Other Canoe Trail Information

The canoe routes that are maintained by the Ontario Department of Lands and Forests are well organized. Each district is responsible for the trails within its boundaries and so can best answer local inquiries. Here are a few canoe trails that are near the upper Midwest.

FORT FRANCIS AREA* Voyageurs' Highway from Lac La Croix to Rainy Lake is eighty miles long, has two portages, and takes four days. Fort Francis to Vermilion Bay via Pipestone Lake, is 100 miles long, has more than twelve portages, and takes ten days.

KENORA AREA** Lake of the Woods contains 12,000 pine-studded islands and has an infinite variety of canoe routes. Manitou Lakes Route is 125 miles long, has 18 portages, and takes twelve days.

SAULT STE. MARIE AREA*** Batchawana River Route is forty miles long, has nine portages, and takes four days. The forty-mile Garden River Route takes two days.

SIOUX LOOKOUT**** Lac Seul Route (Sioux Lookout to Red Lake) is 165 miles long, has seven portages, and takes

---

*Information is available from the district forester, 922 Scott St., Fort Francis, Ontario, Canada.

**The district forester, 808 Robertson St., Kenora, Ontario, Canada, can provide information.

***Contact the district forester, Sault Ste. Marie, 875 Queen St., East, Sault Ste. Marie, Ontario, Canada, for further information.

****The district forester, Box 309, Sioux Lookout, Ontario, Canada, can be consulted for further information.

There are similar listings for other areas, including Geraldton, White River, Sudbury, and Chapleau in the regions a little beyond those mentioned above.

seven to ten days. A trip on the English River from Press Lake to Sioux Lookout is fifty-two miles long, has ten portages, and takes five days.

The Hinterland

North of the canoeing expanses already mentioned, the hinterland beckons. Access to waters that are unreachable by canoe is by bush plane. Reliable bush pilots fly from Fort Francis, Kenora, and other cities and take you to Hudson's Bay Posts. There you will meet the Indians who spend the summer waiting for the long trapping season, when entire families move to fall, winter, and spring hunting camp villages. Such Hudson's Bay posts as Pikangekum, Little Grand Rapids, Deer Lake, and Sandy Lake are not too far away by plane.

The adventure begins when the bush plane lands. Then, paddling away, all your ties with civilization are severed. In the following days of exciting cruising, there will be a confrontation with natural forces and a grappling with the truth of self-reliance known well by the early generations of natives, explorers, missionaries, and settlers.

On the water and along the forested portage paths you will find a primitive character that remains as it was hundreds of years ago. In this experience modern canoeists find high adventure with an impact more stimulating than LSD. The hinterland trip gives insights into the freedom of the Indian, the courage of the explorer, and the sacrifice of the missionary, and the chances are good that you will come to develop these qualities.

HUDSON'S BAY COMPANY It has been said that the Hudson's Bay Company* was the Sears and Roebuck of the hin-

---

*The Northern Stores Department, Hudson's Bay Company, Winnipeg, Manitoba, Canada, can supply additional information. For those interested in knowing the extent and location of posts, a map that indicates the posts scattered throughout the dominion is available.

The bush plane transports crew, equipment, and canoe for pick up
later by appointment.
(Old Town Canoe Company, Old Town, Maine)

terland, stocking every possible basic need of the far-flung
residents—Indians and others. Several wilderness posts
offer a U-Paddle Canoe Rental Service. Canoes for trips
are picked up at one company post, paddled to distant posts,
and dropped off without backtracking—very similar to the
operation of U-Haul cars, trucks, and trailers. Last-minute
grub supplies and general briefings are supplied by the post
managers as they launch modern-day voyagers on their
wilderness adventures. Just visiting and observing the
Hudson's Bay enterprise, which dates back to 1670 and is
synonymous with the fur trade, will serve as an exciting,
interesting experience. The post managers are experienced
outdoorspeople. Outgoing and cooperative, they serve the
hinterland canoeist in a multitude of ways.

This brief discussion of across-the-border canoe experiences will offer stateside canoeists some insights and inspi-
ration into opportunities to enlarge their canoeing horizons.

If you spend some time in Canada, you will identify with friendly neighbors more conditioned to canoeing and the rugged life than we, and perchance some of their expertise and friendship will transfer to us.

Appendix 1

Canoe Rental Directory

As canoeists vary in skill and experience, ranging from the first-timer to the expert, so too canoe trails vary in difficulty. Those intent on a trip to unknown waters should consult with canoe livery personnel for recommendations on waters best suited to their experience and skill.

Livery personnel will arrange any type of trip, from a few hours to several days or weeks. They will furnish all necessary equipment and clue you in to current water conditions. It is important that advance reservations be made, particularly when group cruises require several craft.

Illinois

Outdoor World
629 S. Broadway
Aurora, Illinois 60505

Back Country Outfitting
516 N. Main
Bloomington, Illinois 61701

T & V Marine
9436 W. 47th Street
Brookfield, Illinois 60513

Chockstone Mountaineering, Ltd.
216 S. University Avenue
Carbondale, Illinois 62901

Pirate's Cove Marina
Highway 13—East
Carbondale, Illinois 62901

Robert L. Hardin
1804 Bellamy Drive
Champaign, Illinois 61820

Chicagoland Canoe Base, Inc.
4019 N. Narragansett Avenue
Chicago, Illinois 60634

American Rental Center
1928 Plainfield Road
Crest Hill, Illinois 60435

Charles R. Pickett
2421 Georgetown Road
Danville, Illinois 61832

H_2O Sports, Inc.
716 W. Lincoln
DeKalb, Illinois 60115

Congdon Canoe Company
828 N. Western Avenue
Lake Forest, Illinois 60045

Pack & Paddle, Inc.
701 E. Park Avenue (Route 176)
Libertyville, Illinois 60048

Argyle Lake Concessions
Attn: Bronald L. Mead
908 Jamie Lane
Macomb, Illinois 61455

Waupecan Valley Park
One mi. S. of I-80 on Route 47,
   and two mi. W. on Southmor Road
Morris, Illinois 60450

Timber Lake Resort
Mount Carroll, Illinois 61053

Rock River Recreation
R.R. 2
Oregon, Illinois 61061

Two Rivers Sports Center
U.S. 36 & 54
Pittsfield, Illinois 62363

Zimmerman Canoes
503 Lockport
Plainfield, Illinois 60544

Westwood Camping Center
220 W. Main Street
Plano, Illinois 60545

Merkel's Marine
1720 Broadway
Quincy, Illinois 62301

H_2O Sports, Inc.
2521 S. Alpine
Rockford, Illinois 61108

West Side Marine
2936 S. MacArthur
Springfield, Illinois 62704

Oppold Marina
Stouffer Road
S. of Woodland Road
Sterling, Illinois 61081

The Coho Shop
622 Grand Avenue
Waukegan, Illinois 60085

Wheaton Rental Center
908 E. Roosevelt Road
Wheaton, Illinois 60187

Outdoor Recreation
1515 S. Route 47
Woodstock, Illinois 60098

Indiana

Elmer's Marine Sales
Route 5, Crooked Lake
Angola, Indiana 46703

Nordberg Rent-All Store
340 S. Washington Street
Bloomington, Indiana 47401

Lantz's Canoe Rental
c/o Brookville Marine
10 W. 4th Street
Brookville, Indiana 47012

Morgan's Brookville Canoe Center
Box 118, Route 2—Blue Creek Road
Brookville, Indiana 47012

Whitewater Valley Canoe Rentals, Inc.
Route 52, P.O. Box 2
Brookville, Indiana 47012

Lon-Cha Canoe Center
13733 Wicker Avenue
Cedar Lake, Indiana 46303

Tom's Canoe Rental
Box 173
Cedar Grove, Indiana 47106

Clements Canoes Rental & Sales
Robert J. Clements
911 Wayne Avenue
Crawfordsville, Indiana 47933

U-Rent-It-Center, Inc.
1317 Darlington Avenue
Crawfordsville, Indiana 47933

Ernie's Canoes
5517 W. 133rd Street
Crown Point, Indiana 46307

Canoes from Kendall's Inc.
1919 N. "B" Street
Elwood, Indiana 46036

Fishermen's Headquarters & Canoe Outfitting
209-223 E. Sheridan Street
Ely, Minnesota 55731

Graystone Canoe Trip Outfitters
1829 E. Sheridan
Ely, Minnesota 55731

Kawishiwi Lodge (on Lake One)
Box 480
Ely, Minnesota 55731

Pipestone Outfitting Company
P.O. Box 780
Ely, Minnesota 55731

Quetico Superior Canoe Outfitters
Box 89
Ely, Minnesota 55731

Bill Rom's Canoe Country Outfitters
629 E. Sheridan Street
Ely, Minnesota 55731

Wilderness Outfitters, Inc.
1 E. Camp Street
Ely, Minnesota 55731

Arrowhead Waters Canoe Outfitters
Box A
Grand Marais, Minnesota 55604

Bearskin Lodge & Canoe Trail Outfitters
East Bearskin Lake
Grand Marais, Minnesota 55604

Beartrack Outfitting Co.
Grand Marais, Minnesota 55604

McCann's Canoe Sales & Rental
200 Main Street
Cornell, Wisconsin 54732

Buoy Marine, Inc.
3115 E. Layton Avenue
Cudahy, Wisconsin 53110

Camp One
Route 1, Box 606
Danbury, Wisconsin 54830

Rick's Log Cabin, Inc.
Star Route 1, Box 10
Danbury, Wisconsin 54830

Sportsmen's Park
Paul & Carole Brahm
P.O. Box 551
Delavan, Wisconsin 53115

Norby's Sport Shop
U.S. Highway 63
Drummond, Wisconsin 54832

Vespies Lodge
Lake Owen
Drummond, Wisconsin 54832

Boat-S'-Port
R.R. 3 (3 mi. E. of Eagle River on Highway 70)
Eagle River, Wisconsin 54521

Deerskin Resort and Campground
R.R. 3 (4 mi. N. of Eagle River on Highway 45,
    E. 4 mi. to Chain Lakes Road)
Eagle River, Wisconsin 54521

Currier's Lake Aire Motel
Route 4, Box 414
Rice Lake, Wisconsin 54868

Ron's Southgate Sport Shop
1822 S. Main
Rice Lake, Wisconsin 54868

Richland Canoe Sales and Rentals
Bill's Mobil Service
Highway 14
Richland Center, Wisconsin 53581

The Voyageurs Canoe Outfitters
Box 582 (Highway 87 & U.S. 8)
St. Croix Falls, Wisconsin 54024

Clarke's Sport Shop
Highway 70
St. Germain, Wisconsin 54558

Marawaraden Resort
Route 1 (Long Lake)
Sarona, Wisconsin 54870

Blackhawk Ridge
Box 92 (Highway 78 S.)
Sauk City, Wisconsin 53583

Sauk Prairie Canoe Rental
106 Polk Street
Sauk City, Wisconsin 53583

"W" Sport Shop
2 mi. W. of Sayner
Sayner, Wisconsin 54560

Olson Canoe Rental
c/o Roderick Olson
Kickapoo River
Soldiers Grove, Wisconsin 54655

Bob's River Side Camp
R.R. 2 (Wisconsin River)
Spring Green, Wisconsin 53588

Otter Lake Resort
Route 2 (S. end of Otter Lake)
Stanley, Wisconsin 54768

DuBay Marina
R.R. (Highway 51 at the point where
   crosses Lake Dubay on south shore)
Stevens Point, Wisconsin 54481

Quam's Marine
Highway 51
Stoughton, Wisconsin 53589

Northwest Outlet, Inc.
1815 Belknap
Superior, Wisconsin 54880

Aero Marine
2½ mi. E. of Three Lakes on Highway 32
Three Lakes, Wisconsin 54562

Shorewood Marine
(3 mi. E. of Three Lakes on Highway 32)
Three Lakes, Wisconsin 54562

Three Lakes Marina
(1 mi. N. of Three Lakes on Highway 45)
Three Lakes, Wisconsin 54562

Tomahawk Trailer & Boat Sales, Inc.
Highway 51 N.
Tomahawk, Wisconsin 54487

Canfield's Resort and Campgrounds
Namekagon River
Trego, Wisconsin 54888

Wild River Canoe Rental and Sales
John Kaas
Route 1
Trego, Wisconsin 54888

E. Z. Rental Service
1320 S. West Avenue
Waukesha, Wisconsin 53186

Ding's Dock, Inc.
Route 1, Highway Q
Waupaca, Wisconsin 54981

River Boat Rental
Route 3
Waupaca, Wisconsin 54981

Edmund's Boat Line
Route 1
Waupaca, Wisconsin 54981

Prell's Boat Livery
Route 1
Waupaca, Wisconsin 54981

Lake of the Woods Campgrounds
Route 1, Box 207
Wautoma, Wisconsin 54982

Marineland, Inc.
7105 W. North Avenue
Wauwatosa, Wisconsin 53213

Kickapoo Canoe Rental
c/o Paul Morel
Box 238 (Wisconsin & Kickapoo & Mississippi Rivers)
Wauzeka, Wisconsin 53826

Appendix 2

Information and Map Directory

"500,000 Miles of Canoe & Hiking Routes." Available from the Ohio Canoe Adventures, 5128 Colorado Avenue, Box 2092, Sheffield Lake, Ohio 44054.

"Index Map of U.S. Government Quadrangles." Available from Clarkson Map Company, 725 DesNoyer Street, Kaukauna, Wisconsin 54130.

"Midwest Canoe Livery Guide." Available from the Illinois Paddling Council, 2316 Prospect Avenue, Evanston, Illinois 60201.

"Quimby's Guide." Revised and updated annually, this guide is valuable for canoeists cruising the upper Mississippi River and its tributaries. Available from Box 85, Prairie du Chien, Wisconsin 53821.

"Rent-A-Canoe Directory." Lists over 900 locations nationwide. Available from Ed Nelson, Grumman Boats, Marathon, New York 13803.

"Wilderness Sports Map Outfitting Service." In-depth mapping service for the hinterland canoeist, explorer, fisher, or hunter. Available from Eagle Valley, New York 10974.

Designated Rivers
1. St. Croix River, Wisconsin, Minnesota   10-2-68
2. Wolf River, Wisconsin   10-2-68
3. Lower St. Croix, Wisconsin, Minnesota   10-25-72

Proposed Rivers
4. Upper Mississippi, Minnesota
5. Kettle, Minnesota
6. Upper Iowa, Iowa
7. Wisconsin, Wisconsin
8. Manistee, Michigan
9. Pere Marquette, Michigan
10. Au Sable, Michigan

Midwestern National River System.

Appendix 3

National Wild and Scenic River System (NWSRS)

Stateside canoeists are heartened by the NWSRS, established October 2, 1968, to preserve some of our remaining wild rivers, preserving them in their natural, free-flowing state, free from the threat of dams, pollution, and other assault.

The bill, originally proposed by Senator Frank Church of Idaho, protects the area 300 feet on either side of the waterways to keep the rivers primitive and undeveloped, avoiding commercialism that would destroy the scenic values along the riverbanks. After considering many rivers, the original committee established an initial system including eight, only two of which are in the Midwest: the St. Croix in Wisconsin and Minnesota and the Wolf in Wisconsin. Then in 1972 the lower St. Croix was added.

Of the twenty-seven possible additions to the system identified by Congress, to date only nine of the required studies have been completed, twelve are nearing completion, and six are still in early stages. Canoeists and conservationists were actively engaged in urging more money and momentum for the NWSRS. Some results have accrued; in 1973 several strengthening amendments to the act were approved by Congress, and a year later twenty-nine rivers were added for studied consideration. The act further encourages the inclusion in the system of rivers that have been designated by state legislatures as wild, scenic, or recreational and which meet all criteria.

The Bureau of Outdoor Recreation is currently conducting a "national inventory" of other rivers to determine which are appropriate for study for inclusion into the system. All of us are challenged to nominate favorite stretches of water. To qualify, the water must be a river segment that is free-flowing, and at least twenty-five miles long, and the adjacent shorelines must be relatively free of development.

A comprehensive guidebook on wild and scenic rivers, describing the federal system, giving the status of state systems, and explaining how citizens can effectively contribute to wild and scenic river systems and other means of river preservation will be available soon (River Conservation Fund, 317 Pennsylvania Avenue S.E., Washington, D.C. 20003).

Index